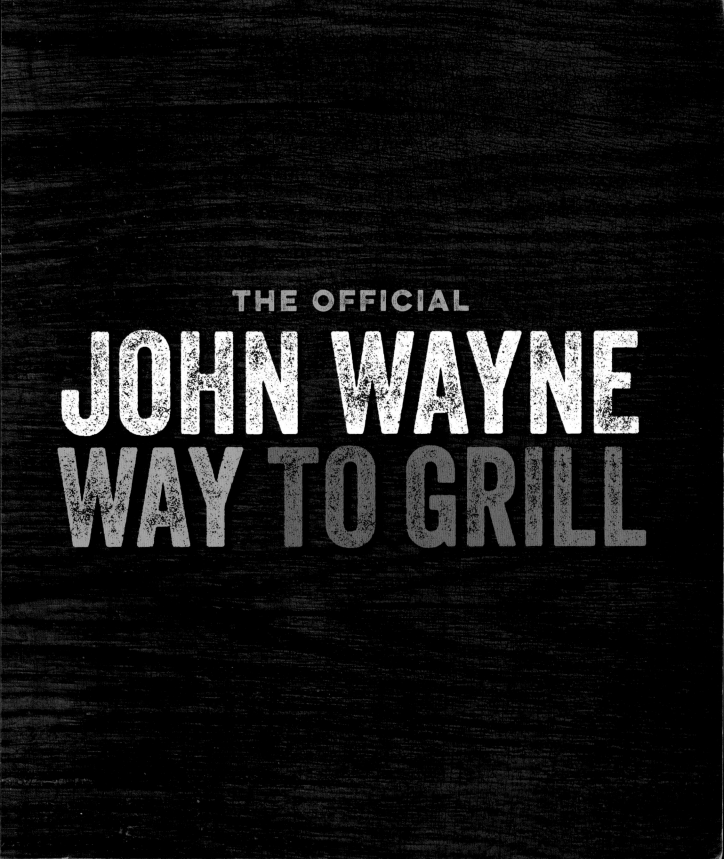

THE OFFICIAL

JOHN WAYNE
WAY TO GRILL

THE SEARCH IS OVER

There are lots of cookbooks out there, but this is the only grill guide you'll need. It's a lot like *The Searchers*: A definitive work that ups the ante for anything that might come after it.

MY FATHER WAS A BIG MAN WITH AN APPETITE TO MATCH.

But before he was a big man, he was a little boy who didn't have the means to eat steak. As a boy, he usually had to make do with peanut butter on saltine crackers for his lunch. So by the time he could afford to eat steak, he never looked back. My father would have eaten steak and potatoes at every meal, and the phrase "charred medium" still rings in my ears. As much as he enjoyed a well-prepared piece of meat, what John Wayne loved best about a meal was how it brought us all together. Gathered around the grill, trading stories and laughs, a dinner at the end of a long day of work meant good times and better company. I'm pleased to share with you this collection of recipes and techniques, as well as some Wayne family tips for how to get the most out of a bite to eat. Whether you're a tenderfoot behind the grill or an old hand, there's something here for everyone—delivered with Duke's trademark no-nonsense style. My father wasn't big on cookbooks, but I'm confident this is one he'd approve of.

Dig in.

Ethan Wayne

— **ETHAN WAYNE**

TABLE OF CONTENTS

GRABBING A MOUTHFUL
Duke enjoying a John Wayne-sized serving of sausage. Sausage is great for anyone grilling in a hurry, especially if you split them open lengthwise, which reduces cook time to five minutes.

GRILLING BASICS

IT'S A SIMPLE CONCEPT: FIRE PLUS MEAT EQUALS DINNER. BUT IT CAN BE HARROWING TO THE UNINITIATED. USE THESE TRICKS, AND GRILL LIKE DUKE.

Lighting Your Grill

First, remove all ash and grease from your grill. A brush with metal bristles will scrape up all the charred fat and remove last month's flavors from your grill. If you don't have a grill brush, don't fret. You can use aluminum foil by crumpling it into a ball and handling it between your tongs. Next, add some charcoal. The amount you'll use will vary depending on the size of your grill, but as a rule of thumb, try to make two full, even layers of briquettes. Once you've got your layers, stack them into a cone shape in the middle of your grill. In stormy or windy weather, you'll want to use a few more briquettes so your grill stays nice and hot. Next, pour lighter fluid on the coals, paying special attention to the middle of the cone. Use about a quarter-cup of lighter fluid (60ml) per pound (450g) of charcoal. Wait about 30 seconds for the lighter fluid to soak into the charcoal, then light with a long match or compact roll of newspaper.

Keeping Your Grill Perfect

Perfect, for grilling purposes, means hot, clean and lubricated. This will minimize outside flavors imparted by the grill and maximize the quality of your meal. In addition to preheating and cleaning your grill as just described, using a paper towel covered in oil can go a long way toward keeping your grill slick and minimizing the sticky, charred remains that tend to linger after you've served up the grub. Simply place the paper towel in your tongs and rub the grill with oil before you start cooking.

Direct or Indirect Heat

Before you start cooking, you'll have to make a decision between direct and indirect heat. Foods that take less than 30 minutes to cook over flame are best cooked directly. These include boneless chicken, steaks, fish fillets, hamburgers and hot dogs. All you really have to do is toss them on the grill and try not to torch them. Foods that take longer than 30 minutes are best grilled with indirect heat. Whole turkeys, bone-in chicken, brisket and other larger fare should be placed above a drip pan to create an effect similar to oven-roasting. If you're using charcoal, arrange your briquettes on the lower level against the drip pan before placing your meat on the grill. You can add water to the drip pan to provide some extra moisture, or get a little creative if you like and add something like apple juice for a bit of flavor.

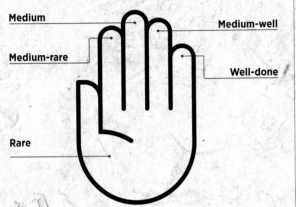

No Thermometers

Sure, you could use a fancy probe thermometer to ensure you've got the temperature just right. But you can also use the thermometer God gave you: your hands. If you're cooking 1-inch slices of steak, rare meat will take about 15 to 20 minutes over a 350° grill—if you can only stand to hold your hand over the coals for around 7 seconds, it's cooking at 350°. At this temperature, a steak cooked to medium will be done in less than 25 minutes and a well done one can take up to 30. To check the temperature of the meat, hold your hand down flat and push your thumb into the fleshiest part of the palm (see chart above). The softness of that spot will mimic the feel of a rare steak. Next, touch your thumb to the pads of each of your other fingers. By moving from the index finger to the pinky, you can compare the feel to that of a medium rare, medium, medium well and well-done steaks, in turn. And remember: You can always toss a steak back on the grill to bring it to a higher temperature—but you can't un-cook charbroiled meat.

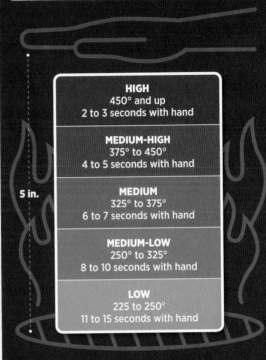

TAKING TEMPERATURES

For the recipes in this book, consult this handy guide.

5 in.

HIGH
450° and up
2 to 3 seconds with hand

MEDIUM-HIGH
375° to 450°
4 to 5 seconds with hand

MEDIUM
325° to 375°
6 to 7 seconds with hand

MEDIUM-LOW
250° to 325°
8 to 10 seconds with hand

LOW
225 to 250°
11 to 15 seconds with hand

Most of the recipes in this book recommend a grilling temperature which you can gauge using the old school method: hold your hand 5 inches above the grate until you can't stand the heat. The chart above gives you a temperature range based on how long you can keep your hand above the grate. Don't put your hand closer than 5 inches.

Putting Out the Fire

After covering your grill, close the vents and allow your coals to burn out. Then let the ashes cool for at least 48 hours and dispose of them in a container that isn't flammable. If you absolutely have to cut that 48 hours short, remove each brick individually with long tongs and submerge them either in water or sand.

ESSENTIALS

GET THESE GOODS TO BECOME THE UNQUESTIONABLE MASTER OF YOUR GRILL.

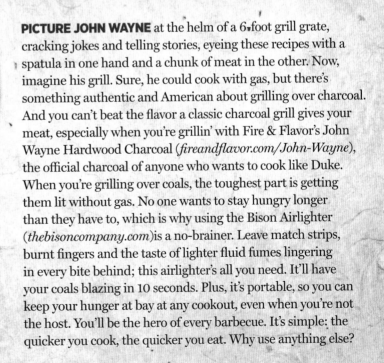

PICTURE JOHN WAYNE at the helm of a 6-foot grill grate, cracking jokes and telling stories, eyeing these recipes with a spatula in one hand and a chunk of meat in the other. Now, imagine his grill. Sure, he could cook with gas, but there's something authentic and American about grilling over charcoal. And you can't beat the flavor a classic charcoal grill gives your meat, especially when you're grillin' with Fire & Flavor's John Wayne Hardwood Charcoal (*fireandflavor.com/John-Wayne*), the official charcoal of anyone who wants to cook like Duke. When you're grilling over coals, the toughest part is getting them lit without gas. No one wants to stay hungry longer than they have to, which is why using the Bison Airlighter (*thebisoncompany.com*)is a no-brainer. Leave match strips, burnt fingers and the taste of lighter fluid fumes lingering in every bite behind; this airlighter's all you need. It'll have your coals blazing in 10 seconds. Plus, it's portable, so you can keep your hunger at bay at any cookout, even when you're not the host. You'll be the hero of every barbecue. It's simple: the quicker you cook, the quicker you eat. Why use anything else?

**BETTER THAN GOOD
GUACAMOLE**
PAGE 25

STARTERS

Break out these apps while you man the grill to get your barbecue off on the right foot.

Spinach Artichoke Dip

Pilar's Souffle

Cheesy Pigs in a Blanket

Grilled Chicken Nachos

Better than Good Guacamole

Ugly Cheddar Biscuits with Garlic Butter

Ma's Meatballs

Homemade Hummus

Grilled Texas Toast

Classic Midwest Cheese Ball

Bacon-pinned Peppers

Warm Turnip Green Dip

Beef and Asparagus Bundles

SPINACH ARTICHOKE DIP

Spinach artichoke is the John Wayne of dips. You know what you're gonna get going in—and it's a bona fide crowd pleaser.

PROVISIONS

- 1 (10-oz.) package frozen spinach, thawed and chopped
- 1 (14-oz.) can artichoke hearts, drained and chopped
- ⅔ cup sour cream
- 1 cup cream cheese
- ¼ cup mayonnaise
- ¾ cup grated Parmesan cheese
- ½ tsp. garlic powder
- ½ cup Parmesan cheese
- 2 tsp. minced garlic
- Crushed red pepper, optional

PREP

1. Preheat oven to 375°.

2. Combine all ingredients until well mixed.

3. Bake for 20 to 30 minutes or until done to your liking. Serve while warm with the dipping selection of your choice, including crushed red pepper flakes for spice.

The Original Duke

As a boy, John Wayne was so inseparable from his pet dog, an Airedale terrier named Duke, that local firefighters took to calling him "Little Duke," and the nickname stuck.

PILAR'S SOUFFLE

Duke's wife Pilar often made this side when he went on location. He kept the recipe on him, cooking it for others on set. With a base of cheese and chilies, it's great for breakfast, lunch or dinner.

PROVISIONS

- 1 lb. Monterey Jack cheese, grated
- 1 lb. cheddar cheese, grated
- 2 (4-oz.) cans green chilies, drained, seeded and diced
- 4 eggs, separated
- 1 tbsp. flour
- ⅔ cup evaporated milk
- ½ tsp. salt
- ⅛ tsp. pepper
- 2 medium tomatoes, sliced and halved

PREP

1. Lightly oil or spray a 10- or 12-inch Dutch oven.

2. Layer cheeses and chilies in bottom of oven.

3. Beat egg yolks slightly, then mix with flour, milk and seasonings. Beat whites until soft peaks form, then fold into yolk.

4. Spread evenly over cheese layer in Dutch oven. Form an overlapping border around the edge of the dish with tomatoes, pushing slices halfway into mixture.

5. Bake at 325° for 30 to 40 minutes.

DID YOU KNOW?

This may seem like a lot of cheese, but the cheddar and Monterey Jack melt with the chilies to make this egg souffle perfectly proportional.

Duke and Pilar enjoy each other's company
during one of their many vacations in Hawaii.

CHEESY PIGS IN A BLANKET

This new and improved twist on a classic is perfect to debut at your barbecue. Thanks to the cheese inside these pigs' blankets, they'll be devoured as soon as you bring them out.

PROVISIONS

1 (8-oz.) tube crescent rolls

8 hot dogs, cut into thirds

¼ cup shredded Monterey Jack cheese

Parmesan cheese

Garlic salt

PREP

1. Preheat oven to 375°. Roll out crescent rolls, placing 2 triangles together and pinching together at the seam. Cut each crescent square that you formed into 6 strips.

2. Sprinkle Monterey Jack cheese on the inside of each strip, then sprinkle them with as much or as little Parmesan and garlic salt as you want. Wrap each strip around a chunk of hot dog.

3. Set the pigs in a blanket on a baking pan and bake for 10 to 12 minutes or until crescents are brown.

WAYNE FAMILY TIP

For any recipe calling for Monterey Jack, you can sub out the popular cheese for it's spicier cousin, Pepper Jack. It'll add a robust, spicy kick to anything from burgers to grits to mashed potatoes.

19

GRILLED CHICKEN NACHOS

A mash-up from both sides of the border, nachos are a welcome addition to the party, no matter who the host is.

PROVISIONS

5 cups tortilla chips

12 oz. boneless grilled chicken, cut into bite-sized chunks (about 4.5 cups)—try the recipe on pg. 84

2 cups finely shredded Monterey Jack cheese

2 tsp. taco seasoning mix

2 tomatoes, finely chopped

3 jalapeños, chopped

2 medium green onions, sliced

1 (15-oz.) can sliced olives

½ cup salsa

Sour cream (optional)

PREP

1. Prepare your grill for medium heat.

2. Spread tortilla chips in pan.

3. Combine chicken, cheese and taco seasoning; spoon evenly over chips. Top with tomatoes, jalapeños, onions, olives and salsa. Sprinkle more cheese on the nachos and cover your pan with foil.

4. Place pan on grill over medium heat. Cover grill and cook for 8 to 10 minutes or until cheese melts. Remove foil with tongs and serve. Top with sour cream if you like.

Duke signs an autograph for a young fan. He always took time to thank those who loved his films.

BETTER THAN GOOD GUACAMOLE

Fresh guacamole is one of the highlights of any trip south of the border, but that doesn't mean you can't do the dish justice yourself. Just make sure your avocados are ripe and soft.

PROVISIONS

- 2 avocados
- 1 onion, finely chopped
- 1 clove garlic, minced
- 1 ripe tomato, chopped
- 1 lime, juiced
- 1 jalapeño pepper, seeded and minced
- 1 tbsp. chopped cilantro

  Salt and pepper

PREP

1. Peel and mash your avocados in a resealable bowl. Stir in the next six ingredients and add salt and pepper to taste.

2. Cover and refrigerate for about an hour. Serve.

Big Fan

Duke was admired all over the world, but he gave as good as he got from an adoring public. He had autograph cards made so that no fan would go without a token of his appreciation, even if he was in a hurry.

UGLY CHEDDAR BISCUITS
WITH GARLIC BUTTER

Because these biscuits are packed with tons of delicious cheese, they'll expand as they cook, losing their shape. But who cares what they look like when they taste this great?

PROVISIONS

BISCUITS

1	cup flour
1¼	tsp. baking powder
½	tsp. salt
¾	cup grated cheddar cheese
	Pinch of Parmesan cheese
2	tbsp. butter
⅔	cup milk

BUTTER

1	stick butter, melted
¼	tsp. garlic powder
¼	tsp. salt
¼	tsp. pepper
⅛	tsp. dried parsley flakes
1	tsp. chopped chives

PREP

1. Preheat oven to 450°.

2. For biscuits, combine first five ingredients and cut butter into the mixture until coarse crumbs form. Using a fork, stir milk into flour mixture until a dough forms. Just be sure not to over-mix it.

3. Drop teaspoons of dough onto an ungreased baking sheet about 1 inch apart. Bake for 15 minutes.

4. Make the butter while your biscuits are baking. Mix all your ingredients in a bowl and keep the mixture warm.

5. Once your biscuits are baked, serve the warm butter on top or as a side for folks who like to do things themselves.

WAYNE FAMILY TIP

Baking is more chemistry than art, and temperature is important. Make sure your butter is cold when you add it into your mixture, and you'll get flaky biscuits every time.

MA'S MEATBALLS

Bet you didn't know you could make meatballs with only five ingredients. It's so easy a kid—like Duke or his younger brother Robert, left, with their mother—could do it.

PROVISIONS

1 (20-oz.) package ground beef

2 tbsp. olive oil

1 egg

⅔ cup Italian seasoned bread crumbs

1 small onion, chopped

PREP

1. Combine all ingredients and shape into about 20 meatballs. The bigger the meatball, the longer it'll take to cook.

2. Preheat oven to 400°. Put meatballs in 9x13 pan and cook for 20 to 30 minutes or until browned and cooked through. For a little extra flavor, roll your meatballs in barbecue or marinara sauce.

HOMEMADE HUMMUS

You can dip anything in hummus, and with this garlicky recipe, you'll want to. Veggies, pretzels, bread—if you can name it, chances are that it'll taste great with this garbanzo bean-based dip.

PROVISIONS

- **1 (15-oz.) can chickpeas, rinsed**
- **2 cloves garlic**
- **¼ cup olive oil**
- **2 tbsp. lemon juice**
- **¼ tsp. paprika**
- **Salt and pepper**

PREP

1. Throw your first four ingredients in a food processor and blend them. You want your finished product to be smooth, so add water as needed to make that happen.

2. Scoop the mixture from the food processor into a serving bowl. Add as much salt and pepper as you want and top with paprika for a little extra flavor and flair.

WAYNE FAMILY TIP

Using canned chickpeas is quick and easy, but cooking them yourself makes for better-tasting hummus. Soak the chickpeas in cold water the night before, rinse them in the morning and then cook them, covered, in a pot filled with plenty of new water, for about 45 minutes.

GRILLED TEXAS TOAST

Serving bread to kick off a meal is a no-brainer, but this Texas toast will exceed everyone's expectations. Cooked on the grill, coated with garlic butter and sprinkled with cheese, this toast will make plain ol' rolls seem like chopped liver.

PROVISIONS

- 2   loaves white bread, cut into 1-inch-thick slices
- 2   sticks butter, softened
- 8   cloves garlic, pureed
-     Salt and pepper
-     Monterey Jack cheese

PREP

1. Mix butter and garlic together in a bowl, adding salt and pepper to taste.

2. Brush both sides of the bread with the mixture and put the bread on the grill. Grill each side of bread for 1 to 2 minutes or until it turns a light golden brown.

3. Right before you pull bread from grill, add a pinch of cheese if you want. When it melts, move the toast to a plate and serve.

DID YOU KNOW?

Although Duke wasn't born in Texas, some of his greatest films were made there, including *Rio Bravo* (1959), *The Alamo* (1960) and *The Sons of Katie Elder* (1965).

John Wayne stars beside Dean Martin and Ricky Nelson in 1959's *Rio Bravo*.

TOAST OF THE TOWN
John Wayne, playing Captain Rockwell W. "Rock" Torrey in the film *In Harm's Way* (1965), raises a glass to his brothers in arms. While Duke would share a drink with anyone who met his standards as a straight shooter and standup guy, the invitation list for his Christmas parties read like a *Variety* front page and included names such as Clint Eastwood and Henry Fonda.

CLASSIC MIDWEST CHEESE BALL

Pair this can't-miss app with the crackers of your choice and watch your guests line up to ask you if you're planning on serving any more.

PROVISIONS

2	(8-oz.) packages cream cheese, softened
1	(1-oz.) package ranch dressing mix
2½	cups shredded cheddar cheese
1	tsp. Worcestershire sauce
1	tsp. garlic powder
3	small green onions, chopped
1½	cups chopped pecans

PREP

1. Mix all ingredients except pecans in bowl, using a handle mixer set on low.

2. Scoop out entire mixture onto a serving platter and start to form it into a sphere with your hands.

3. Cover your cheese ball with chopped pecans. Surround the end result with the crackers of your choice and serve, adding a knife for easy spreading.

Cultural Icon

"Westerns are closer to art than anything else in the motion picture business," Duke once said. *In order to keep Western art alive, Duke donated substantially to the National Cowboy & Western Heritage Museum in Oklahoma City.*

John Wayne shares laughs with military men during one of his morale-boosting visits.

BACON-PINNED PEPPERS

If you're feeling adventurous, replace your sweet peppers with jalapeños. The heat level may be too unpredictable for everyone to enjoy—but that just means more for you.

PROVISIONS

2   pints miniature sweet peppers

12 hickory-smoked bacon slices

1   (8-oz.) container garlic-and-herb spreadable cheese

8   (5- by 3-inch) disposable aluminum bread pans

PREP

1. Heat grill to medium-high. Cut 1/2 inch from stem end of each pepper. Remove and discard seeds and membranes.

2. Cut bacon slices in half crosswise. Microwave, in 2 batches, at high for 90 seconds or until bacon is partially cooked.

3. Improvise a pastry bag by spooning cheese into a 1-qt. zip-top plastic bag. (Do not seal.) Snip one corner of bag to make a small hole. Pipe cheese into the cavity of each pepper, filling almost full.

4. Place one bacon half over cut side of each pepper, securing with a wooden toothpick.

5. Carefully cut three 1-inch holes in bottom of each loaf pan. Turn pans upside down; place peppers, cut sides up, in holes in pans.

6. Grill peppers in pans, covered, over medium-high heat for 6 to 8 minutes or until bottoms of peppers are charred and bacon is crisp.

Man of Action

Duke went out of his way to show his appreciation for our troops. One night a group of servicemen on leave rowed a boat to his house but got cold feet before knocking on the door and debated leaving. Duke heard the commotion and invited the soldiers in for a drink.

WARM TURNIP GREEN DIP

Although the recipe is cooked in a Dutch oven, you can transfer the dip to a 1- or 2-qt. slow cooker set on warm so guests can enjoy this creamy dip throughout the day. To make it spicier, serve with extra crushed red pepper and your favorite brand of hot sauce on the side.

PROVISIONS

- 5 **bacon slices, chopped**
- ½ **sweet onion, chopped**
- 2 **cloves garlic, chopped**
- ¼ **cup dry white wine**
- 1 **(16-oz.) package frozen chopped turnip greens, thawed**
- 12 **oz. cream cheese, cut into pieces**
- 1 **(8-oz.) container sour cream**
- ½ **tsp. dried crushed red pepper**
- ¼ **tsp. salt**
- ¾ **cup freshly grated Parmesan cheese**

PREP

1. Cook bacon in a Dutch oven over medium-high heat for 5 to 6 minutes or until crisp; remove bacon and drain on paper towels, reserving 1 tbsp. drippings in Dutch oven.

2. Sauté onion and garlic in hot drippings for 3 to 4 minutes. Add wine and cook for 1 to 2 minutes, stirring to loosen particles from bottom of Dutch oven. Stir in turnip greens, next four ingredients and 1/2 cup Parmesan cheese. Cook, stirring often, for 6 to 8 minutes or until cream cheese is melted and mixture is thoroughly heated. Transfer to a lightly greased 1 1/2-qt. baking dish. Sprinkle evenly with remaining 1/4 cup Parmesan cheese.

3. Broil 6 inches from heat for 4 to 5 minutes or until cheese is lightly browned. Sprinkle evenly with bacon.

Presidential Pal

Duke was friends with several Commanders-in-Chief, including Gerald Ford and Ronald Reagan. A lifetime Republican, Duke called himself a member of the "loyal opposition" in a letter congratulating Jimmy Carter on his electoral victory.

BEEF AND ASPARAGUS BUNDLES

These bundles are diet friendly—but so packed with flavor that no one would ever know—and they look great on a serving tray. Given their short prep time, you're sure to get more credit than you deserve when you break these out at your next barbecue.

PROVISIONS

16 asparagus spears

1 (4-oz.) package garlic-and-herb spreadable cheese

2 heads Bibb lettuce, leaves separated

8 thin slices deli roast beef, halved

1 red bell pepper, cut into 16 strips

16 fresh chives (optional)

PREP

1. Snap off and throw out the tough ends of asparagus. Cut asparagus tips into three 1/2-inch pieces.

2. Cook asparagus in boiling water, covered, for 1 to 2 minutes or until crisp-tender; drain. Dunk into ice water to stop the cooking process; drain and pat dry with paper towels.

3. Spoon cheese into a 1-qt. zip-top plastic bag. Don't seal it. Improvise a pastry bag by snipping one corner of the bag to make a small hole and pipe cheese down center of each lettuce leaf. Arrange one roast beef slice, one asparagus spear and one red bell pepper strip in each lettuce leaf. If desired, wrap sides of lettuce around roast beef and vegetables and tie bundles with chives.

WAYNE FAMILY TIP

Rather than try to get an accurate headcount for how much you'll need in the starter department, always overshoot it. You can pack up what's left over for lunches or snacks for the rest of the week.

John Wayne stars as Jim Gordon in one of his very first war films, *Flying Tigers* (1942).

BLACK-AND-BLUE STEAKS
PAGE 75

Classic and straightforward, steak was John Wayne's favorite, and these recipes exemplify everything he loved about it.

The Perfect Porterhouse

Miso-Marinated Skirt Steak

Grilled Beef Skewers with Moroccan Spices

Hamburger Steak with Sweet Onion-Mushroom Gravy

Spice-Rubbed Flank Steak with Spicy Peach-Bourbon Sauce

Hickory Grilled Tenderloin with Sweet and Spicy Steak Sauce

Curried Beef Kebabs with Jade Sauce

Skirt Steak with Chimichurri

Blue Cheese Beef

Peppered Cowboy Steaks

Down Home Steak Salad

Bacon-Wrapped Filet Mignon

Wild West Strip Steak

Black-and-Blue Steaks

Tennessee T-Bone Steaks with Whiskey Butter

Sesame-Crusted Beef Tenderloin with Hawaiian Relish

THE PERFECT PORTERHOUSE

When it comes to steak, sometimes it's tough to pick your favorite cut. Porterhouse offers the best of both worlds: a bone-in strip sirloin and a portion of tender filet mignon.

PROVISIONS

- 4 (2-inch-thick) porterhouse steaks
- 4 tbsp. olive oil
- 12 tbsp. butter
- Salt and pepper

PREP

1. Rub your steaks with olive oil, then season them with as much or as little salt and pepper as you want.

2. Heat one side of your grill to high, making sure your grates are well-greased. Grill steaks over high heat for 6 minutes. Flip and cook for another 6 minutes or so. Move steak to cool part of grill; cover for 12 to 15 minutes.

3. Pull steaks from grill. Top each steak with 3 tbsp. of butter. Let rest 5 minutes before serving.

WAYNE FAMILY TIPS

End debates about who's the best griller by using these simple tricks.

Make sure your meat's at room temperature before you throw it on the grill. That way, the steaks will cook evenly, and you'll save yourself a struggle.

If you want those iconic grill marks, throw your steaks on the grill and don't touch them until they need to be flipped.

Most of your seasoning will be lost to your grill grates, so don't be afraid to use your spices with gusto.

For the best taste, handle your steaks with tongs. Forks puncture the meat and cost you flavorful juice.

To avoid a plateful of juice, let your cooked steaks sit on a serving plate for about half their cook time. By then, the meat will have rested, soaking up most of that juice, and it'll be ready to eat.

CAST IRON

MISO-MARINATED SKIRT STEAK

Skirt steak is a flavorful cut but tends to be tougher than others. In this miso-marinated recipe, sake acts as a tenderizer.

PROVISIONS

- 1   cup sake
- ¼   cup chopped green onions
- 2   tbsp. brown sugar
- 2   tbsp. miso
- 2   tbsp. rice wine vinegar
- ¼   tsp. freshly ground black pepper
- 2   cloves garlic, minced
- 1   (1-lb.) skirt steak, trimmed

PREP

1. Combine first seven ingredients in a blender; process for 1 minute or until onions are finely chopped. Transfer mixture to a large zip-top plastic bag. Add steak to bag and seal. Marinate in refrigerator for at least 2 hours and up to 8, turning occasionally.

2. Remove steak from bag, reserving marinade. Pat steak dry with paper towels.

3. Heat a large nonstick skillet over medium-high heat. Lightly spray both sides of steak with cooking spray. Add steak to pan; cook 1 minute on each side or until browned.

4. Remove steak from pan; set aside and keep warm. Add reserved marinade to pan and cook for 4 minutes or until thick and deep brown in color, stirring constantly. Return steak to pan, turning to coat. Cook for 2 minutes or to desired degree of doneness. Let steak stand for 5 minutes. Cut steak diagonally across grain into thin slices.

GRILLED BEEF SKEWERS
WITH MOROCCAN SPICES

These savory skewers are the perfect make-ahead summer barbecue food: tons of flavor with none of the fuss so you can focus on the important stuff. Like eating.

PROVISIONS

½	cup chopped fresh parsley	½	tsp. crushed red pepper
½	cup chopped fresh cilantro	1	lb. flank steak, cut into 1-inch by 2-inch pieces
¼	cup chopped fresh mint	¼	red onion, cut into 1-inch pieces
2	tbsp. olive oil		
1	clove garlic	1	red pepper, cut into 1-inch pieces
1	tsp. brown sugar		
1	tsp. salt	1	yellow pepper, cut into 1-inch pieces
1	tsp. lime zest		Lime wedges
½	tsp. ground cumin		

PREP

1. Pulse first 10 ingredients in a food processor until finely minced. Pour into a plastic zip-top bag, add meat and chill for roughly 2 hours.

2. Preheat grill to medium high. Assemble skewers by piercing each piece of steak into a "U" shape and threading peppers and onions. Grill 14 minutes for medium or until meat is caramelized and firm, flipping once. Squeeze lime over each skewer and serve.

CAST IRON

HAMBURGER STEAK
WITH SWEET ONION-MUSHROOM GRAVY

Ground beef is a staple in any man's cuisine. But these hamburger steaks go beyond the standard after you smother them in light, sweet onion-mushroom gravy.

PROVISIONS

- 2 honey-wheat bread slices
- 1 lb. ground round
- 1 large egg, lightly beaten
- 2 cloves garlic, minced
- ½ tsp. salt
- ½ tsp. freshly ground pepper
- 1 (1.2-oz.) envelope brown gravy mix
- 1 tbsp. vegetable oil
- 1 (8-oz.) package sliced fresh mushrooms
- 1 medium sweet onion, halved and thinly sliced

PREP

1. Process bread slices in a food processor for 10 seconds or until finely chopped. Place breadcrumbs in a mixing bowl; add ground round and next four ingredients. Gently mix with your hands until blended. Shape into four 4-inch patties.

2. Whisk together brown gravy mix and 1 1/2 cups water; set aside.

3. Cook patties in hot oil in a large skillet over medium-high heat for 2 minutes on each side or until just browned. Remove patties from skillet. Add mushrooms and onion to skillet and sauté for 6 minutes or until tender. Stir in prepared gravy and bring to a light boil. Return patties to skillet and spoon gravy over each patty. Cover, reduce heat to low and simmer for 8 to 10 minutes.

WAYNE FAMILY TIP

The Cast Iron Skillet

Everyone loves the classic grill lines that come with outdoor grates, but flavor should never be sacrificed to achieve a look. Some of the best steak recipes call for searing in a cast iron skillet. Although these skillet-cooked steak recipes won't yield those picture-perfect grill lines, they'll result in some of the juiciest cuts of meat you've ever eaten. Don't worry, cooking with a cast iron skillet doesn't confine you to the kitchen. You can—and should—throw your skillet directly on the grill and get cooking. You can even forgo the grill rack and place the skillet directly in the coals. Just try to keep the ashes out of your grub.

John Wayne as the iconic character Rooster Cogburn in the sequel to *True Grit* (1969), *Rooster Cogburn* (1975).

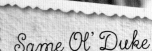

SPICE-RUBBED FLANK STEAK
WITH SPICY PEACH-BOURBON SAUCE

Canned peach nectar, near the bottled fruit juices in the grocery, is the base for a slightly sweet sauce. You can make and refrigerate the sauce up to a day ahead—but make sure to bring it to room temperature before serving.

PROVISIONS

SAUCE

1	tsp. vegetable oil
¾	cup chopped Vidalia or other sweet onion
2	cloves garlic, minced
1½	cups peach nectar
3	tbsp. brown sugar
2	tbsp. cider vinegar
3	tbsp. bourbon
2	tbsp. ketchup
1½	tsp. Worcestershire sauce
½	tsp. crushed red pepper
1	tsp. fresh lime juice

STEAK

1	tbsp. brown sugar
1¼	tsp. garlic powder
1¼	tsp. ground cumin
1	tsp. salt
1	tsp. ground coriander
1	tsp. paprika
¾	tsp. dry mustard
¾	tsp. freshly ground black pepper
2	(1-lb.) flank steaks, trimmed

PREP

1. To prepare sauce, heat oil in a medium saucepan over medium-high heat. Add onion and garlic, sauté for 5 minutes or until tender. Add nectar, 3 tbsp. sugar and vinegar. Bring to a boil and cook until reduced to 1 cup (about 15 minutes). Add bourbon, ketchup, Worcestershire and red pepper; cook over medium heat for 2 minutes, stirring occasionally. Remove from heat and stir in the lime juice. Cool slightly. Pour the sauce into a blender and process until smooth.

2. Prepare grill to cook at medium-high heat.

3. To prepare steak, combine 1 tbsp. sugar and next seven ingredients (through black pepper); rub over both sides of steak. Place steak and cook 7 minutes on each side or to desired degree of doneness. Cut steak diagonally across grain into thin slices. Serve with sauce.

Same Ol' Duke

Winning an Academy Award for Best Actor didn't much change John Wayne. Of his Oscar-winning performance in True Grit *(1969), Duke said, "You can't eat awards. Nor, more to the point, drink 'em."*

HICKORY GRILLED TENDERLOIN
WITH SWEET AND SPICY STEAK SAUCE

This zesty sauce is also great with grilled pork or chicken. Major Grey's chutney is a chunky, spicy Indian condiment; look for it in the supermarket near the steak sauces.

PROVISIONS

SAUCE

- ⅔ cup ketchup
- ½ cup Major Grey's chutney
- ⅓ cup bottled chili sauce
- ¼ cup steak sauce
- ¼ cup Worcestershire sauce
- ½ tsp. hot sauce

BEEF

- 4 cups hickory wood chips
- 2 cups water
- 1 (3¼-lb.) beef tenderloin, trimmed
- 1 tsp. freshly ground black pepper
- ½ tsp. salt

PREP

1. To prepare sauce, combine all six ingredients; cover and chill.

2. Soak wood chips in water for 1 hour.

3. Remove grill rack; set aside. Prepare grill for indirect grilling, heating one side to medium-high and leaving one side unheated.

4. Put half of the wood chips on hot coals. Place a disposable aluminum foil pan on unheated side of grill. Pour 2 cups water in pan. Grease up grill rack.

5. Sprinkle beef evenly with salt and pepper. Place beef on grill rack over foil pan on unheated side. Close lid; cook for 55 minutes or until a thermometer registers 135° or to desired degree of doneness. Add additional wood chips halfway through cooking time.

6. Remove beef from grill. Cover lightly with foil and let stand for 15 minutes. Cut beef across grain into thin slices. Serve with sauce.

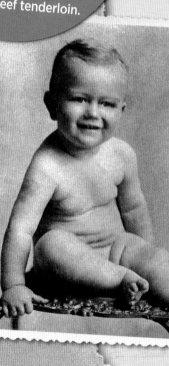

CURRIED BEEF KEBABS
WITH JADE SAUCE

Take ordinary steak kebabs to the next level with this delicious Indian-inspired sauce. Your guests—and taste buds—will thank you.

PROVISIONS

SAUCE

- ½ cup chopped fresh cilantro
- ¼ cup chopped fresh mint
- 2 tbsp. chopped green onions
- ¼ cup extra virgin olive oil
- 1 tsp. grated lime rind
- 1 tbsp. fresh lime juice
- 2 tsp. seeded and minced jalapeño pepper
- 2 tsp. honey
- 1 tsp. minced garlic
- ¼ tsp. salt

KEBABS

- 12 (6-inch) wooden skewers
- 2 tbsp. peanut oil
- 1¼ tsp. garam Masala
- 1¼ tsp. garlic salt
- ¾ tsp. curry powder
- ½ tsp. ground black pepper
- ¼ tsp. ground cumin
- 1½ lb. flat iron steak, cut into 1-inch pieces
- ½ cup sweetened flaked coconut, toasted

PREP

1. Process all sauce ingredients in a food processor for 10 seconds or until thoroughly blended, pausing to scrape down sides as needed.

2. For kebabs, soak wooden skewers in water 30 minutes. Preheat grill to medium-high. Whisk together peanut oil and the next five ingredients in a large bowl until blended. Add steak pieces and toss them around a bit to coat.

3. Thread beef chunks onto skewers. Grill beef, covered with grill lid, over medium-high heat for 3 minutes on each side or to your desired degree of doneness.

4. Place skewers on a serving platter and drizzle with the sauce. Top with flaked coconut if you're feeling fancy.

SKIRT STEAK
WITH CHIMICHURRI

Easy to find and quick to cook, skirt steak is an obvious choice for a spur-of-the-moment cookout. Add this hearty herb sauce for flavor and color.

PROVISIONS

½	cup finely chopped fresh parsley
⅓	cup extra virgin olive oil
¼	cup fresh lemon juice
2	cloves garlic, finely chopped
½	tsp. crushed red pepper or more to taste
	Salt
1½	lb. skirt steak

PREP

1. For chimichurri, mix parsley, oil, lemon juice, garlic, crushed red pepper and 1/4 tsp. salt in a bowl.

2. For the steak, preheat your grill to high and oil when hot. Sprinkle steak with salt. Grill steak for 4 to 6 minutes, flip and continue to cook until the steak reaches your desired degree of doneness.

3. Transfer steak to cutting board, tent loosely with foil and let stand for 5 minutes. Slice and spoon chimichurri on top to serve.

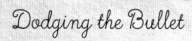

Dodging the Bullet

Although John Wayne was a worldwide superstar, not everyone loved him. Two dictators in particular—Joseph Stalin and Communist China's Mao Tse-tung—attempted to have Duke assassinated. Luckily, their plots were foiled.

John Wayne relaxes for a moment behind the scenes in a chair made specially for him.

CAST IRON

BLUE CHEESE BEEF

A rich, powerful Gorgonzola sauce adds some flavor to tender beef filets. The sauce is so good you might start putting it on everything.

PROVISIONS

- 2 tbsp. butter
- 1 medium onion, thinly sliced
- 1 (8-oz.) package sliced fresh mushrooms
- 1 pint heavy cream
- 4 oz. crumbled Gorgonzola cheese
- 6 (6-oz.) beef tenderloin filets
- ¾ tsp. salt
- ¼ tsp. pepper

  Crumbled Gorgonzola cheese to garnish

PREP

1. Melt butter in a large skillet over medium-high heat. Add onion and cook, stirring often, for 6 to 8 minutes or until tender. Add mushrooms and cook, stirring often, for 5 minutes. Reduce heat to medium and cook 5 more minutes or until mushrooms are tender.

2. Bring cream to a boil in a medium saucepan over medium heat. Reduce heat to low and simmer, stirring often, for 15 minutes or until slightly thickened.

3. Add crumbled cheese to cream and cook, whisking often, over medium heat for 4 minutes or until cheese is melted. Stir in onion mixture; put aside and keep warm.

4. Sprinkle filets with salt and pepper. Sear filets in your skillet over medium-high heat for 5 to 8 minutes on each side or to desired degree of doneness. Remove filets from skillet and let sit for 10 minutes. Top with warm cheese sauce and a little bit of crumbled Gorgonzola.

DID YOU KNOW?

Duke's character dies in less than 5 percent of his 200 or so films. Villains who took his life include Bruce Dern (*The Cowboys*, 1972, above) and a giant squid (*Reap the Wild Wind*, 1942).

PEPPERED COWBOY STEAKS

A bone-in ribeye or "cowboy steak" is a can't-miss cut everybody can agree on. This simple rub of black and red ground peppers, lemon pepper, garlic powder and parsley flakes takes ribeyes from good to extraordinary. One hour in the fridge is all it takes to add even more flavor to these solid standbys.

PROVISIONS

2½	tsp. black pepper
1	tbsp. dried thyme
1½	tsp. salt
4½	tsp. garlic powder
1½	tsp. lemon pepper
1½	tsp. ground red pepper
1½	tsp. dried parsley flakes
6	(1½-inch-thick) bone-in ribeyes
3	tsp. olive oil

PREP

1. Mix first seven ingredients. Brush steaks with oil; rub with pepper mixture. Cover and stick in the fridge for 1 hour.

2. Grill with grill lid shut, over medium-high heat for 8 to 10 minutes on each side or to desired degree of doneness.

WAYNE FAMILY TIP

A bone-in steak will always have a bit more flavor than a cut off the bone. You can cover any exposed bones on your steaks with aluminum foil to keep them from charring as you grill.

John Wayne stars as the revenge-seeking John Wyatt in the 1935 flick *Westward Ho*.

DOWN HOME STEAK SALAD

Beef up your salad—literally. Veggies and steak coexist in this tasty dish, which is made even better by its sweet homemade mustard dressing.

PROVISIONS

SALAD

1	loaf Italian bread, cut into 12 slices
1	clove garlic
1	lb. skirt or flank steak
	Salt and pepper
1	(1-lb.) bag romaine hearts, torn
12	cherry tomatoes, halved

DRESSING

¼	cup sour cream
¼	cup mayonnaise
2	tsp. lemon juice
1	tsp. mustard
1	tbsp. finely chopped fresh parsley
1	clove garlic, chopped
¼	tsp. salt

PREP

1. Preheat broiler to high; set a rack 5 inches from heat. Line a baking sheet with foil. Set bread slices on baking sheet and toast, flipping once, until golden, for 2 to 4 minutes. Rub one side of each slice with one garlic clove.

2. Prepare grill for cooking. Massage steak with salt and pepper. Place steak on well-greased grill and cook for 4 to 6 minutes, flip once, and continue to cook until the steak reaches your desired degree of doneness. Tent with foil and let rest for 5 minutes.

3. Mix lettuce and tomatoes in a large bowl. To make dressing: Whisk together all ingredients, pour on salad, then toss to coat.

4. Divide salad onto 6 plates. Cut steak and add it to salad. Serve with toasted bread.

Picture Perfect

John Wayne loved a good adventure and a new challenge, especially when it came to his career. "Well, you like each picture for a different reason," Duke once said. "But I think my favorite will always be my next one."

BACON-WRAPPED FILET MIGNON

One of Duke's favorite foods, bacon tastes great on everything—including filet mignon. Wrapping these lean pieces of meat in bacon adds fat and flavor and traps in extra moisture.

PROVISIONS

- 4 (10-oz.) cuts of filet mignon
- 8 slices bacon
- 4 tbsp. olive oil
- Salt and pepper
- Fresh rosemary

PREP

1. Heat grill to high.

2. Wrap two pieces of bacon around each filet, keeping the pieces even with the top and bottom of the steaks. Secure bacon with toothpicks.

3. Mix olive oil with desired amount of salt, pepper and rosemary. Massage into your filets, but be careful not to rip apart your bacon in the process.

4. Turn grill down to medium-high heat.

5. Put the steaks on the grill to sear. Close lid. After 3 minutes, flip steaks. Cook for 3 more minutes. Continue flipping steaks until done to your liking. Let rest for 10 minutes, then serve.

Good Eatin'

There was never a bad time for bacon at Duke's house, but mornings were when it was enjoyed most. "At breakfast, he'd have a plate of eggs and a separate plate just piled with crispy bacon," Ethan (pictured) remembers.

Fair Fighter

Although he appeared in more than 200 films, many of them Westerns, John Wayne's characters never once shot an enemy in the back. For his final film, The Shootist (1976), Duke insisted on a rewrite in order to keep this streak intact.

WILD WEST STRIP STEAK

Strip steak is a bit tougher than a cut like filet mignon, but it more than makes up for it with flavor. This quick preparation lets the grill do the work so you can take it easy for once in your life.

PROVISIONS

4 (14-oz.) strip steaks

Extra virgin olive oil

Smoked paprika

Salt and pepper

PREP

1. Rub steaks with olive oil, mashing lightly with your palms. Liberally season steaks with as much smoked paprika, salt and pepper as you want; stick in the fridge, uncovered, for up to 24 hours.

2. Prepare your grill.

3. Toss your steaks on the grill over medium-high heat. Cook for 6 minutes and flip. Cook for 6 more minutes or to your desired degree of doneness.

CAST IRON

BLACK-AND-BLUE STEAKS

Any villain who dared cross John Wayne's on-screen characters typically left the showdown black and blue—if they were lucky. A hard day of fightin' will work up anyone's appetite, and these Pittsburgh-style steaks—black char on the outside, rare temp within—will hit the spot.

PROVISIONS

- 2 (12-oz.) shell steaks
- ¼ tsp. salt
- ⅛ tsp. pepper
- 4 tbsp. butter

PREP

1. The key to a good Pittsburgh steak is high heat. You want to sear the steak until it's crispy without cooking the meat through.

2. Heat your cast iron skillet over the grill until it's searing hot.

3. Season steaks with salt and pepper.

4. Add butter to the skillet, then toss in steaks. Cook for 5 minutes or until nice and crisp. When steaks stop sizzling, flip them. Cook for another 5 minutes.

5. Remove from heat and let rest for 8 minutes before serving.

DID YOU KNOW?

To win a bet with longtime friend and co-star Ward Bond (below in 1957's *The Wings of Eagles*), John Wayne once punched him in the face through a closed door.

RIDING THE RANGES
Duke in a scene from the movie *Flame of Barbary Coast* (1945). John Wayne used to ride his horse Jenny to elementary school as a child and grew up to be an accomplished horseman.

TENNESSEE T-BONE STEAKS
WITH WHISKEY BUTTER

T-bone steaks come from the short loin and have huge flavor. Often, this cut tastes best when you let that flavor shine through and don't clutter it up with a bunch of fancy seasonings. The whiskey butter is a side you can throw on the meat as a garnish or serve with fresh bread or biscuits. It's a meal fit for Davy Crockett.

PROVISIONS

STEAK

2	(1½-inch-thick) T-bone steaks
2	tsp. salt
1	tsp. black pepper

BUTTER

½	cup butter, softened
2	tbsp. whiskey
1	tbsp. white wine vinegar
1	tbsp. Worcestershire sauce
2	tsp. Dijon mustard
¼	tsp. salt
¼	tsp. cayenne pepper

PREP

1. Bring grill to medium heat.

2. Cover both sides of your room-temperature steaks with salt and pepper. Put steaks on grill and cook for 9 to 11 minutes, flipping once.

3. For butter, mix all the ingredients together until well blended. Pack into a bowl using wax paper, cover and chill until you're ready to serve.

SESAME-CRUSTED BEEF TENDERLOIN STEAKS
WITH HAWAIIAN RELISH

Embrace multiple flavors with these delicious tenderloin steaks, perfectly paired with a better-than-it-should-be tropical relish filled with some of Hawaii's best fruits.

PROVISIONS

RELISH

½ cup finely chopped pineapple

½ cup finely chopped peeled mango

¼ cup finely chopped red bell pepper

2 tbsp. chopped fresh cilantro

1 tbsp. fresh orange juice

½ tsp. grated orange rind

½ tsp. crushed red pepper

STEAK

½ tsp. salt

½ tsp. freshly ground black pepper

4 (4-oz.) beef tenderloin steaks (about 1 inch thick)

4 tsp. black sesame seeds

PREP

1. To prepare relish, combine all seven ingredients in a bowl; set aside.

2. For the meat, heat grill to medium-high. Sprinkle salt and pepper evenly over steaks. Coat both sides of each steak with 1/2 tsp. sesame seeds, pressing gently to stick. Throw steaks on grill and cook for 5 minutes on each side or to your desired degree of doneness. Serve with relish.

Hawaiian Highlights

Many of John Wayne's movies were set and shot in Hawaii, allowing Duke to become friends with local legends such as Hawaiian surfer Duke Kahanamoku, one of the pioneering athletes of his day. The two even starred together in the 1948 film Wake of the Red Witch (above).

**MARINATED GRILLED
CHICKEN LEGS**
PAGE 93

CHICKEN

Chicken's good for your body and your wallet, and these simple,
delicious recipes will be good for your cookout.

The Best Darned Grilled Chicken Ever

Asian Barbecue Chicken

Desert Heat Herb-Rubbed Grilled Chicken

Chicken Kebabs with Must-Have Dippin' Sauce

Marinated Grilled Chicken Legs

Rosemary Chicken Thighs with Spinach and Cheese Grits

Grilled Chicken and Two-Bean Salad

Grilled Chipotle Chicken Quesadillas

Grilled Tequila Chicken

Thai Chicken Sandwich

Grilled Chicken with Rustic Mustard Sauce

Grilled Chicken with White Barbecue Sauce

California-Style Grilled Chicken Rolls

Home of the Brave BBQ Chicken

Can't-Miss Chicken Thighs with Sweet Onions and Peppers

Lemon Chicken with Fresh Corn Cakes

THE BEST DARNED GRILLED CHICKEN EVER

That's no lie! This recipe brings together a wide variety of spices to give the chicken uniquely irresistible flavor.

PROVISIONS

- 5 tbsp. Cajun meat seasoning blend
- 1¼ tsp. ground cardamom
- 1 tbsp. plus 1 tsp. onion powder
- 1 tbsp. plus ¾ tsp. ground ginger
- 1 tbsp. grated lemon peel
- 1 tbsp. grated lime peel
- 1¼ tsp. ground cinnamon
- 1¼ tsp. ground nutmeg
- 1¼ tsp. ground savory
- ¾ tsp. ground allspice
- ¾ tsp. ground dried guajillo or pasilla chile pepper (½ pepper)
- 1 tbsp. plus 1½ tsp. soy sauce
- 1 (3- to 4-lb.) chicken, cut into 8 pieces
- 4 bay leaves
- ¼ cup unsalted butter

PREP

1. Combine first 11 ingredients in a large bowl. Remove 1/4 cup mixture and set aside. Add soy sauce to remaining seasoning and stir well to form a paste. Place chicken pieces and bay leaves in a large bowl and rub chicken evenly with paste. Cover tightly with plastic wrap and stick in the fridge for 6 to 8 hours.

2. Remove chicken from refrigerator about 1 ½ hours before grilling so it reaches room temperature. Melt butter and stir in reserved 1/4 cup seasoning mixture. Set aside.

3. Prepare a hot fire by piling charcoal on one side of grill, leaving the other side empty (if using a gas grill, light only one side.) Place chicken pieces over cooler side and grill with lid closed, for 25 minutes for breasts and 30 minutes for thighs and legs.

4. Transfer chicken to hot side and grill, flipping several times and basting with reserved butter mixture, until internal temperature reaches 175° or about 7 ½ minutes per side for breasts, 3 ½ minutes per side for thighs and 2 ½ minutes per side for legs. Remove from grill and let stand 10 minutes before serving.

A man of many talents,
Duke mastered chopsticks.

ASIAN BARBECUE CHICKEN

The marinade for these grilled chicken thighs is finger-licking good, and the hits of sweetness and spice are sure to make this dish a crowd-pleaser.

PROVISIONS

- ¼ cup firmly packed brown sugar
- ¼ cup soy sauce
- 1 tbsp. fresh lime juice
- ½ tsp. crushed red pepper
- ¼ tsp. curry powder
- 3 cloves garlic, minced
- 8 (6-oz.) chicken thighs, skinned
- Lime wedges (optional)
- Green onion tops (optional)

PREP

1. Mix first six ingredients in a large zip-top plastic bag and add chicken. Seal and marinate in refrigerator for 4 hours, flipping every now and again.

2. Prepare your grill.

3. Remove chicken from bag and put marinade in a small saucepan. Bring to a boil and cook for 1 minute.

4. Set chicken on grill rack. Grill for 20 minutes or until done, flipping and basting with the marinade often. For presentation's sake, serve with lime wedges and green onion tops.

WAYNE FAMILY TIP

To extinguish a grill fire, your best bet is to close the top of your grill. The lid will limit the amount of oxygen feeding the fire and help eliminate a flare-up.

DESERT HEAT HERB-RUBBED GRILLED CHICKEN

John Wayne was a notorious lover of all things spicy, and this rub delivers the goods and then some.

PROVISIONS

- **1 tsp. onion powder**
- **1 tsp. garlic powder**
- **1 tsp. dried oregano**
- **½ tsp. salt**
- **½ tsp. cayenne pepper**
- **½ tsp. freshly ground black pepper**
- **4 (6-oz.) chicken breast halves**

PREP

1. Preheat your grill to medium-high heat.

2. Combine first 6 ingredients in a small bowl. If you want more kick, feel free to double the cayenne and sub white pepper for the black.

3. Sprinkle spice mixture evenly over both sides of chicken, pressing lightly to stick. The secret to a good rub is to actually rub it into your meat, so don't be afraid to get your hands dirty. If you've got the time, let them sit in the fridge for roughly 30 minutes before tossing them on the grill.

3. Place chicken on a grill rack that's greased up and ready to go; grill 6 minutes on each side or until done.

4. Serve with a cold beer or, for those who can't handle the heat, a glass of milk.

Monumental Scenery

The vast American desert landscape of Monument Valley was the location used to shoot some of John Wayne's most memorable films, including Stagecoach, She Wore a Yellow Ribbon and The Searchers (above).

CHICKEN KEBABS
WITH MUST-HAVE DIPPIN' SAUCE

Kebabs offer something for everyone. Your pals can pick and choose their favorite chunks of meat and veggies—but with this delicious recipe, they'll want it all, particularly when they taste the sauce you're serving up.

PROVISIONS

- ½ cup canola oil
- ½ cup plus 1 tbsp. lemon juice (from about 3 lemons)
- 4 tsp. cumin
- 2 tsp. ground coriander
- 2 tsp. paprika
- 4 cloves garlic, smashed
- 3 lb. boneless, skinless chicken breasts, cut into 1-inch pieces
- 2 red bell peppers, seeded, cut into 1-inch pieces
- 3 small zucchini, cut into 1-inch pieces
- 3 small summer squash, cut into 1-inch pieces
- 1 cup plain Greek yogurt
- 2 tbsp. tahini
- 2 red onions, halved, each half cut into quarters
- Cooked brown rice (optional)
- Salt and pepper to taste

PREP

1. In a bowl, mix oil, 1/2 cup lemon juice, cumin, coriander, paprika and garlic; pour half into a separate bowl. Add chicken to one bowl; turn to coat. Toss peppers, zucchini and squash in the other bowl. Cover bowls and stick in the fridge for at least 2 hours.

2. To make sauce, whisk yogurt, tahini, 1 tbsp. lemon juice and 1/2 tsp. salt in a bowl. Cover and chill.

3. Preheat grill to medium-high. Remove chicken and vegetables from marinade and pat dry. Thread chicken, vegetables and onions onto 12 skewers. Season kebabs with salt and pepper.

4. Grease up grill. Grill kebabs, flipping occasionally, until chicken is cooked through or 4 to 6 minutes. Serve over brown rice, if desired, with sauce.

A Man, a Plan, a Canal

The Government of Panama gifted John Wayne an island, called Isla Taborcillo, off the country's coast, to thank him for his public defense of the small nation. Wayne wrote numerous letters to President Carter in support of the Panama Canal Treaty.

MARINATED GRILLED CHICKEN LEGS

Soy sauce and fresh citrus juices deliver major flavor to tender chicken legs. With a dish like this, everybody's gonna want a drumstick.

PROVISIONS

- 1 cup fresh orange juice
- 2 tbsp. fresh lemon juice
- 4 tsp. soy sauce
- 1 tbsp. dry sherry
- 1½ tsp. bottled garlic, minced
- 1½ tsp. balsamic vinegar
- 1½ tsp. basil oil
- 1 tsp. onion powder
- 1 tsp. dark sesame oil
- ½ tsp. salt
- ¼ tsp. hot pepper sauce
- 8 skinless chicken drumsticks (about 2¼-lb. total)
- Green onion strips (optional)

PREP

1. Put the first 11 ingredients in a large zip-top plastic bag. Add chicken to bag and seal. Marinate in refrigerator for 2 hours, flipping bag occasionally.

2. Prepare grill.

3. Remove chicken from bag, reserving marinade. Put reserved marinade in a small saucepan and cook over medium heat for 3 minutes. Place chicken on grill that's greased and ready to go; grill for 30 minutes or until chicken is done, flipping and basting occasionally with reserved marinade. Top with onion strips.

ROSEMARY CHICKEN THIGHS

WITH SPINACH AND CHEESE GRITS

These sweet and spicy marinated thighs will wow even your most hard-to-impress guests. And if they don't, more for you.

WAYNE FAMILY TIP

Toss rosemary directly on your coals to add extra flavor to your food. Added bonus: The scent repels mosquitoes.

PROVISIONS

CHICKEN

1	clove garlic, pressed
1	tbsp. olive oil
2	tbsp. Dijon mustard
2	tbsp. honey
1	tsp. salt
1	tsp. chopped fresh rosemary
½	tsp. pepper
1½	lb. boneless, skinless chicken thighs
½	lemon

SAUTÉED GARLIC SPINACH

1	clove garlic, pressed
1	tbsp. olive oil
1	bag (10 oz.) fresh spinach

TWO-CHEESE GRITS

1	cup uncooked quick-cooking grits
1	cup (4 oz.) shredded cheddar cheese
½	cup (2 oz.) shredded Parmesan cheese
2	tbsp. butter

PREP

1. Combine garlic and next six ingredients in a large heavy-duty zip-top plastic bag. Squeeze bag to combine ingredients. Add chicken, flip to coat and seal bag. Chill for at least one hour.

2. Preheat grill to medium-high. Remove chicken from marinade; discard marinade.

3. Grill chicken with lid down over medium-high heat for 5 to 7 minutes on each side. Transfer to a large piece of aluminum foil and squeeze juice from lemon over chicken; fold foil around chicken, covering chicken completely. Let stand 10 minutes.

SAUTÉED GARLIC SPINACH

1. Heat 1 tsp. olive oil in a nonstick skillet over medium-high heat. Sauté one pressed garlic clove in hot oil for 30 seconds.

2. Add spinach, thoroughly washed, to skillet and cook for 2 to 3 minutes or until spinach is wilted. Sprinkle with salt and pepper to taste. Serve spinach with slotted spoon or tongs. Makes four servings.

TWO-CHEESE GRITS

1. Bring 4 cups water and 1 tsp. salt to a boil in a 3-quart saucepan. Whisk in 1 cup grits; reduce heat to medium-low and cook for 5 to 6 minutes or until tender.

2. Remove from heat and stir in 1 cup (4 oz.) shredded cheddar cheese, 1/2 cup (2 oz.) shredded Parmesan cheese and 2 tbsp. butter. Salt and pepper to taste.

GRILLED CHICKEN AND TWO-BEAN SALAD

This healthy, hearty chicken- and bean-filled salad is the perfect power meal for when you've worked up a Duke-sized appetite.

PROVISIONS

¾ lb. green beans, trimmed, cut into bite-size pieces

¼ cup extra virgin olive oil

1 tbsp. Dijon mustard

1 tbsp. red wine vinegar or sherry vinegar

1 small shallot, finely chopped (about 2½ tbsp.)

1 pint cherry tomatoes, halved

1 (14-oz.) can white beans, drained

1 lb. boneless, skinless chicken breasts

Salt and pepper to taste

PREP

1. Combine green beans and 1 cup lightly salted water in a microwave-safe bowl; cover. Microwave on high until beans are crisp-tender or about 4 minutes. Drain.

2. In a bowl, whisk 3 tbsp. oil along with mustard, vinegar, 1/2 tsp. salt and shallots. Add green beans, tomatoes and white beans and toss until coated.

3. Preheat grill to high. Brush chicken with remaining 1 tablespoon oil; sprinkle with salt and pepper. Grill, covered, until chicken is cooked through, flipping once, 8 to 10 minutes total. Let cool slightly and chop.

4. Add chicken to the bowl with the rest of the ingredients, toss and serve.

WAYNE FAMILY TIP

Want to add a little flavor without using a heavy sauce? Smoke halved lemons over a low grill flame for 2 minutes and juice them into your salad dressing.

John and Patrick Wayne on the
set of *Rio Bravo* (1959).

GRILLED CHIPOTLE CHICKEN QUESADILLAS

Grilling chicken adds a smoky flavor—the perfect complement to bold flavors like lime, cilantro and chile.

PROVISIONS

PICO DE GALLO

- 2 cups diced tomatoes
- ½ cup diced onion
- 2 tbsp. minced jalapeño chiles
- ¼ cup minced fresh cilantro
- 2 tbsp. fresh lime juice
- 1 tsp. garlic
- Salt

QUESADILLAS

- 4 boneless, skinless chicken breast halves
- 1 tbsp. olive oil
- 1 canned chipotle chile in adobo sauce, drained and minced
- ¼ cup sour cream
- ¼ cup mayonnaise
- 1 tbsp. lime juice
- 1 tbsp. chopped fresh cilantro
- 8 (6-inch) corn tortillas
- 2 cups grated Monterey Jack cheese
- Salt and freshly ground black pepper

PREP

1. For pico de gallo, mix tomatoes, onion, jalapeño chiles, cilantro, lime juice and garlic in a bowl. Add salt to taste.

2. Brush chicken breasts with olive oil and sprinkle with salt and pepper. Place chicken on grill over medium heat or put chicken in a grill pan over medium heat. Cook for 4 to 5 minutes per side or until cooked through (cut to check). Slice cooked chicken breasts into 1/4-inch-thick slices. Keep grill or grill pan hot.

3. In a small bowl, whisk together chipotle chile, sour cream, mayonnaise, lime juice and cilantro.

4. Spread 1 tbsp. mixture on each of the tortillas. Top four of the tortillas each with 1/2 cup cheese and a quarter of the chicken slices, then cover with the remaining tortillas, sauce side down. Put each quesadilla on a dinner plate.

5. Slide quesadillas off plates onto the grill over medium heat or slide into a grill pan over medium heat (you may need to grill the quesadillas in batches). Grill uncovered, turning once, until cheese is melted and both sides are golden or about 2 minutes on each side (use a large spatula and tongs to flip the quesadillas). If grilling in batches, keep finished quesadillas warm in a 200° oven until ready to serve.

6. Slice each quesadilla into wedges and serve with homemade pico de gallo on the side.

GRILLED TEQUILA CHICKEN

Create an amazing blend of flavors by marinating the chicken in a mixture of lime juice, fresh ginger, dried chipotle chile and one of Duke's favorite spirits: tequila. You can also stir the marinade into whipped heavy cream for a rich, savory topping.

PROVISIONS

- 4 boneless, skinless chicken breast halves
- ½ cup garlic-infused olive oil
- 2 tbsp. tequila
- 2 tbsp. fresh lime juice
- 1½ tsp. hot sauce
- 1 tsp. Worcestershire
- 1 tsp. grated fresh ginger
- 1 tsp. ground dried chipotle chile
- 1 tsp. salt
- ⅓ cup heavy whipping cream
- Cilantro (optional)

PREP

1. Pound chicken to 1/4-inch thickness. In a bowl, whisk oil, tequila, lime juice, hot sauce, Worcestershire, ginger, chile and salt. Reserve 1/3 cup of marinade, then put the chicken in bowl, flip and marinate for 30 minutes.

2. Grill chicken over medium heat, flipping once, until cooked through or 6 to 8 minutes total.

3. In a small saucepan over medium-high heat, simmer reserved marinade until reduced to 1/4 cup or about 2 minutes. Whisk in cream, then remove from heat. Serve chicken topped with sauce and cilantro.

More Than a Hobby

Duke's favorite way to pass the time was with a game of chess. Whether he was on set between takes, at home or relaxing on the Wild Goose, *more often than not he had a game of chess going—with a glass of añejo tequila on the side. He even played correspondence matches via the post.*

Duke ponders his next move
in an intense chess match.

THAI CHICKEN SANDWICH

This spicy sandwich is rounded out with a creamy peanut sauce. Onion sprouts add just the right bite.

PROVISIONS

SAUCE

- 2 tbsp. peanut butter
- 2 tsp. soy sauce
- 1½ tsp. dark sesame oil
- 1 tsp. water
- 1 tsp. rice vinegar
- 1 clove garlic, minced

CHICKEN

- ½ cup finely chopped green onions
- 1 tbsp. chile paste with garlic
- 2 tsp. fresh ginger, peeled and grated
- 2 tsp. soy sauce
- ¼ tsp. salt
- 1 lb. boneless, skinless chicken breasts, chopped
- 4 (2-oz.) sandwich rolls with sesame seeds
- 1 cup onion sprouts

PREP

1. For the sauce, mix all six ingredients, stirring with a whisk until smooth.

2. Prepare grill.

3. You'll be forming the chicken into patties, similar to burgers. Put onions and next five ingredients in a food processor, processing them until ground well. Shape mixture into four patties.

4. Place patties on grill, cooking 4 minutes on each side or until done. Put rolls on the grill for 1 minute or until toasted. Place one patty on bottom half of each roll; top patties with 1/4 cup sprouts and about 1 tbsp. sauce. Top with remaining roll halves.

DID YOU KNOW?

One of Duke's favorite roles was that of father to his seven children. "My father would make you feel special when he spent time alone with you," Ethan (above) says.

GRILLED CHICKEN
WITH RUSTIC MUSTARD SAUCE

Creamy Dijon mustard and a dash of rosemary lend moist, tender chicken a delicious, backwoods flavor.

PROVISIONS

- 1 tbsp. plus 1 tsp. Dijon mustard, divided
- 1 tbsp. olive oil
- 1 tsp. chopped fresh rosemary
- ¼ tsp. salt
- ¼ tsp. black pepper
- 4 (6-oz.) boneless, skinless chicken breast halves
- 3 tbsp. mayonnaise
- 1 tbsp. water
- Rosemary sprigs (optional)

PREP

1. Get your grill ready to go.

2. Mix 1 tsp. mustard, oil and next three ingredients in a small bowl. Brush mixture evenly over chicken. Place chicken on greased grill rack and grill for 6 minutes on each side or until done.

3. While chicken grills, mix 1 tbsp. mustard, mayonnaise and 1 tbsp. water in a bowl. Serve mustard cream with grilled chicken. Garnish with rosemary sprigs, if you're feeling fancy.

GRILLED CHICKEN
WITH WHITE BARBECUE SAUCE

Tired of the same old sweet, tomato-based barbecue sauce? Try this Southern-style, tangy mayonnaise-based white sauce, and you may never go back to the red stuff.

PROVISIONS

SAUCE

1½	cups mayonnaise
¼	cup white wine vinegar
1	clove garlic, minced
1	tbsp. coarse ground pepper
1	tbsp. spicy brown mustard
1	tsp. sugar
1	tsp. salt
2	tsp. horseradish

CHICKEN

1	tbsp. dried thyme
1	tbsp. dried oregano
1	tbsp. ground cumin
1	tbsp. paprika
1	tsp. onion powder
½	tsp. salt
½	tsp. pepper
10	chicken thighs (3 lb. total)

PREP

1. For sauce, stir together all sauce ingredients until well blended. Store in an airtight container in refrigerator for up to one week.

2. For chicken, combine first seven ingredients. Rinse chicken and pat dry, then rub mixture evenly over chicken. Place chicken in a zip-top plastic bag, seal and refrigerate for 4 hours. Remove chicken from bag.

3. Grill chicken, covered, over medium-high heat for 8 to 10 minutes on each side. Serve with sauce.

DID YOU KNOW?

Duke was first billed as John Wayne in the 1930 Western *The Big Trail*, in which he played rustic fur-trapper Breck Coleman. It was also his first leading role.

CALIFORNIA-STYLE GRILLED CHICKEN ROLLS

These chicken rolls are perfect for a quick lunch or a casual dinner on a warm summer night. They can be made with leftovers you might have after preparing one of our other recipes—assuming you have leftovers.

PROVISIONS

- 4 (10-inch) flour tortillas
- ¼ cup mayonnaise
- 4 medium leaves Boston lettuce
- 8 oz. boneless grilled chicken, cut into thin, long strips (about 3 cups)—try the recipe on pg. 84
- 1 small cucumber, seeded, peeled and coarsely shredded
- 2 carrots, peeled and coarsely shredded
- 1 ripe avocado, peeled, pitted and cut into 1/2-inch slices
- ¼ tsp. kosher salt
- Freshly ground pepper to taste

PREP

1. Spread mayonnaise on tortillas. Arrange lettuce, chicken, cucumber, carrots and avocado in a line off-center (try not to overstuff). Season with salt and pepper and roll into snug cylinders. Cut into 1 1/2-inch-long rolls and serve. Stick a toothpick in each roll to hold it together.

DID YOU KNOW?

Duke's experience playing football at the University of Southern California helped him get his start. His first flick was a football film called *Brown of Harvard*.

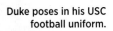

Duke poses in his USC football uniform.

John Wayne starring in *El Dorado* (1966).

HOME OF THE BRAVE BBQ CHICKEN

You've never had barbecue like this before. This sauce—made with ketchup, brown sugar, Worcestershire sauce and mustard—puts the store-bought stuff to shame.

PROVISIONS

- 3 tbsp. butter or oil
- 2 onions, chopped
- 1 clove garlic, chopped
- 1 cup ketchup
- ½ cup chopped celery
- 3 tbsp. packed brown sugar
- 1 tsp. Worcestershire sauce
- 1 tsp. dry mustard
- Salt and pepper to taste
- 6 tbsp. fresh lemon juice
- 16 pieces assorted chicken (breasts, drumsticks, thighs and wings)

PREP

1. Melt butter over medium heat in a medium saucepan. Add onions and garlic and cook, stirring, until onions begin to brown or about 7 minutes. Stir in 1 cup water, ketchup, celery, brown sugar, Worcestershire sauce and mustard. Season with salt and pepper to taste. Bring to a boil, then simmer, stirring occasionally, for 30 minutes. Stir in lemon juice. Set aside 1 cup sauce for a final basting.

2. Grill chicken skin side down on a rack set 5 to 6 inches over glowing coals for 10 minutes, flipping once. Grill for 10 minutes longer, turning once and basting with sauce, until juices run clear when skin is pierced with a paring knife and sauce is nicely browned but not burned (breasts may take up to 10 minutes longer). Move chicken to a platter and use a clean brush to baste well with reserved sauce.

DID YOU KNOW?

Guns were more than props to Duke. They were pieces of history that brought order to the West. He spent years filling his gun collection with beautifully crafted pieces.

John Wayne spends quality time with daughter Aissa.

CAN'T-MISS CHICKEN THIGHS
WITH SWEET ONIONS AND PEPPERS

Sweet, slow-cooked onions and red peppers—combined with Port, capers and thyme—make these grilled chicken thighs a flavor powerhouse.

PROVISIONS

¼	cup extra virgin olive oil
2	red onions, thinly slivered lengthwise
1½	lb. sweet peppers (red bell or Gypsy), stemmed, seeded and slivered lengthwise
½	cup ruby Port
⅓	cup capers, drained
3	tbsp. chopped fresh thyme leaves
12	(6- to 8-oz.) chicken thighs
¼	cup chopped Italian parsley
	Salt and pepper

PREP

1. In a large pan over medium heat, warm the olive oil. Add onions and peppers, cover and cook, stirring occasionally, until very juicy and almost soft or 16 to 20 minutes. Add Port, capers and thyme; stir often, uncovered, until all the liquid has evaporated and vegetables are soft, sweet and beginning to brown, 25 to 35 minutes longer. Remove from heat and season with salt and pepper to taste.

2. Up to 2 hours before serving, in an 8- to 10-quart pan over high heat, bring about 3 quarts water to a boil. Rinse chicken, remove excess fat and place in boiling water. Return water to a boil, then cover, reduce heat and simmer until meat is no longer pink in the center of thickest part (cut to test) or about 15 minutes. Remove chicken from water, drain and pat dry. Reserve broth for another use.

3. Sprinkle both sides of chicken with salt and pepper. Place thighs, skin down, on an oiled grill over a solid bed of medium-high coals or medium-high heat on the grill; cover grill.

4. Cook chicken, flipping once, until browned on both sides or 5 to 9 minutes total. Transfer to a platter. Spoon onion-pepper mixture over chicken and sprinkle with parsley.

LEMON CHICKEN
WITH FRESH CORN CAKES

Start with a package of cornbread mix and fresh corn kernels to make these homestyle corn cakes. Top with grilled chicken, bacon and chopped arugula for a satisfying one-dish dinner.

WAYNE FAMILY TIP

To keep your meat from sticking, use tongs to rub your grill grates with a paper towel soaked in olive oil. Never use cooking spray—you could lose your eyebrows from a flare up.

PROVISIONS

- 3   lemons
- 2   cloves garlic, pressed
- ⅓   cup plus 1 tbsp. olive oil
- 1   tsp. Dijon mustard
- ¼   tsp. pepper
- 1½   tsp. salt, divided
- 3   boneless, skinless chicken breasts
- 3   ears fresh corn, husks removed
- 1   (6-oz.) package buttermilk cornbread mix
- ¼   cup fresh basil, chopped
- 8   thick hickory-smoked bacon slices, cooked
- 2   cups arugula, loosely packed

PREP

1. Preheat grill to medium-high heat. Grate zest from lemons to equal 1 tbsp. Cut lemons in half and squeeze juice from lemons into a measuring cup to equal 1/4 cup.

2. Whisk together lemon zest, lemon juice, garlic, next three ingredients and 1 tsp. salt. Reserve 1/4 cup lemon mixture. Pour remaining lemon mixture in a large zip-top plastic bag and add chicken. Seal and chill for 15 minutes, flipping once. Remove chicken and discard marinade.

3. Brush corn with 1 tbsp. olive oil and sprinkle with remaining 1/2 tsp. salt.

4. Grill chicken and corn at the same time, lid closed, for 20 minutes, turning chicken once and turning corn every 4 to 5 minutes. Remove chicken and cover.

5. Hold each grilled cob upright on a cutting board and carefully cut downward, cutting kernels from cob.

6. Stir together cornbread mix and 2/3 cup water in a small bowl until smooth. Stir in basil and 1 cup grilled corn kernels. Pour about 1/4 cup batter for each corn cake onto a hot, lightly greased griddle. Cook cakes for 3 to 4 minutes or until tops are covered with bubbles and edges look dry and cooked; turn and cook other side.

7. Thinly slice chicken. To serve, place two corn cakes on each plate and top with chicken and two bacon slices. Toss arugula with reserved lemon mixture. Place arugula on bacon and sprinkle with extra corn kernels.

BROWN SUGAR-RUBBED SALMON
PAGE 125

FISH

John Wayne loved the open water as much as he loved the Wild West.
Follow these recipes to grill up the catch of the day.

Grilled Fish Tacos with Homemade Relish

Brown Sugar-Rubbed Salmon

Grilled Fish with Garden Salsa

Wasabi-Infused Mahi Mahi Sandwiches with Napa Slaw

Grilled Halibut with Lemon-Mint Rub

Sunset Halibut with Fresh Mango Salsa

Upscale Scallops with Tomato Sauce and Short Pasta

Jamaican-Style Swordfish Steaks

Fresh Trout Fillets topped with Citrus Crunch

Grilled Wild Salmon with Mushroom Sauce and Roasted Beets

Grilled Shrimp with Tarator Sauce

Southwest Grouper Sandwich with Chipotle Tartar Sauce

GRILLED FISH TACOS
WITH HOMEMADE RELISH

The great thing about a burger is that you can eat it with your hands. The same goes for tacos, which aren't necessarily the first thing you think of when you're talking about grilling out. But these no-fuss grilled fish tacos are easy to cook and feature a tomato-green onion relish that provides a fresh, tangy flavor.

PROVISIONS

RELISH

2	cups tomatoes, chopped
¼	cup sliced green onions
1	jalapeño chile, seeded and minced
¼	cup chopped fresh cilantro
1	tbsp. fresh lime juice
¼	tsp. salt
	Lime wedges (optional)

FISH

1	tbsp. fresh lime juice
2	tsp. canola oil
2	cloves garlic, minced
2	tsp. chili powder
¾	tsp. ground cumin
¼	tsp. salt
¼	tsp. freshly ground black pepper
⅛	tsp. ground cayenne pepper
1	lb. firm white fish fillets
8	(6-inch) whole wheat tortillas

PREP

1. For relish, combine ingredients in a bowl and stir well.

2. For fish, combine first eight ingredients in a bowl. Add fish to bowl; toss to coat.

3. Wrap tortillas in foil. Place fish and tortillas on a well-greased grill rack. Grill fish with the lid on, over medium-high heat for 3 minutes on each side or until it flakes easily with a fork.

4. Divide fish among tortillas and top with relish. Serve with lime wedges.

BROWN SUGAR-RUBBED SALMON

Brown sugar isn't just for baking. When grilled, the brown sugar-paprika rub turns slightly crusty and caramelizes, giving the salmon a flavor and texture that'll have you wishing you'd made twice as much.

PROVISIONS

- 1   cup firmly packed brown sugar
- ½   cup paprika
- ¼   cup kosher salt
- 2   tbsp. dried thyme
- 1   (2-lb.) salmon fillet, cut into portions

PREP

1. Combine first four ingredients. Coat both sides of the salmon with the rub; let sit 10 minutes.

2. Grill salmon over medium-high heat 3 to 4 minutes on each side or to desired degree of doneness. If you want, garnish with thyme.

WAYNE FAMILY TIP

Be careful when removing the salmon's pin bones. Ripping them upward and outward tears the fish's flesh. Instead, use a set of tweezers to pull the bones out in their natural direction.

GRILLED FISH
WITH GARDEN SALSA

If you're looking for a simple way to spice up just about any grilled white fish, top it with this homemade salsa that's brimming with fresh vegetables and a touch of heat, courtesy of a fresh jalapeño pepper. This versatile dish works with any type of mild, firm white fish fillets.

PROVISIONS

- 1½ tsp. ground cumin, divided
- ½ tsp. salt, divided
- 1 tsp. grated lime rind
- 2 tbsp. fresh lime juice
- 1 tbsp. olive oil
- 1 cucumber, chopped
- 1 cup grape tomatoes, halved
- 1 green onion, thinly sliced
- 1 jalapeño pepper, seeded and minced
- 1 tbsp. chopped fresh mint
- 1 lb. mild, firm white fish fillets

PREP

1. Combine 1 tsp. cumin, 1/4 tsp. salt, lime rind, lime juice and olive oil in a medium bowl. Add cucumber, tomatoes, green onion, jalapeño and mint; set salsa aside.

2. Toss remaining 1/2 tsp. cumin and 1/4 tsp. salt over fish. Grill over medium-high heat for 7 minutes or until tender.

3. Top with salsa and serve. You can make the salsa any time and keep it in the fridge 'til company comes over and you're ready to grill, but use it within the week.

WAYNE FAMILY TIP

To create less mess when you grill fish, use aluminum foil instead of a grill pan. That way, come clean-up time, instead of scraping burnt fish skin off your pan while debating whether or not to throw it away, you can just ball up the foil and dump it in the trash.

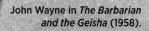
John Wayne in *The Barbarian and the Geisha* (1958).

WASABI-INFUSED MAHI MAHI SANDWICHES
WITH NAPA SLAW

Brown sugar takes some of the bite out of wasabi, creating a flavor-packed sandwich that isn't too fiery. The slaw comes from north of Newport Beach but will be a hit anywhere.

Emperors and Admirers

John Wayne had famous fans around the world. When Japanese Emperor Hirohito visited the United States in 1975, he requested to meet the star, who had spent time in Japan while filming The Barbarian and the Geisha (left) in 1958.

PROVISIONS

- ¼ cup finely minced shallots
- 2 tbsp. finely minced garlic
- 2 tbsp. finely minced ginger
- 2 tsp. wasabi paste
- ½ cup seasoned rice vinegar
- 2 tbsp. tamari
- 2 tbsp. light brown sugar
- ¼ cup toasted sesame oil, divided
- 4 (6-oz.) mahi mahi fillets
- 8 slices ciabatta or 4 rolls, split
- 2 tbsp. tahini
- 1½ cups Napa cabbage, very finely shredded
- 1 cup red cabbage, very finely shredded
- ½ cup carrot, grated
- ¼ cup green onions, chopped
- Mayonnaise

PREP

1. Whisk together the first seven ingredients in a bowl, then whisk in 2 tbsp. sesame oil. Reserve 1/2 cup marinade and set aside. Place fillets in a zip-top plastic bag and add remaining marinade. Seal bag and refrigerate for 1 hour.

2. Remove fish and discard marinade. Grill fish, skin side up, over medium-high heat for 3 to 4 minutes. Flip and grill for 3 to 4 minutes or until fish flakes easily with a fork. Remove and discard skin. Cover and keep warm.

3. Grill bread slices for 3 minutes or until toasted. Set aside.

4. Stir together remaining 2 tbsp. sesame oil and tahini. Stir sesame oil mixture into leftover 1/2 cup marinade.

5. Combine cabbage, carrots and green onion in a bowl. Pour marinade mixture over slaw and toss gently to combine.

6. Lightly spread one side of each bread slice with mayonnaise. Place fish on four pieces of bread; top with slaw and remaining four slices of bread.

The Wild Goose

John Wayne enjoyed spending time with his family and friends on his boat, a decommissioned Navy mine-sweeper dubbed the Wild Goose, *that he transformed into a home away from home. "He loved the fact that, as a young boy, I could drive the small tenders to the* Wild Goose," *his son Ethan says. "If it was windy or rough, my father would tell the crew to 'let the boy bring it in.'"*

GRILLED HALIBUT
WITH LEMON-MINT RUB

There's nothing quite like like catching a massive halibut off the Pacific coast—waters Duke used to roam aboard the *Wild Goose*, from Newport Beach all the way to Alaska. This versatile fish gets a blast of flavor from this bright, mint-infused twist on gremolata, a classic Italian garnish.

PROVISIONS

HALIBUT

4   (6-oz.) halibut fillets

2   tsp. olive oil

½   tsp. salt

½   tsp. freshly ground black pepper

Lemon wedges

LEMON-MINT RUB

3   tbsp. chopped fresh mint

2   tsp. grated lemon rind

1   tsp. finely minced garlic

PREP

1. Brush fillets with oil and toss on some salt and pepper. Place fillets on a grill rack coated with olive oil. Grill with the lid on, over medium-high heat, for 5 minutes on each side or until fish flakes easily with a fork.

2. Combine all ingredients for lemon-mint rub in a small bowl; stir well.

3. Place fillets on individual serving plates and cover evenly with lemon-mint rub. Serve with lemon wedges.

SUNSET HALIBUT
WITH FRESH MANGO SALSA

This sweet and tangy dish is the perfect meal for a warm summer night. The colorful mango salsa is fantastic with halibut but works well with other types of fish, too. Feel free to add extra heat with a teaspoon of cayenne.

PROVISIONS

2	cups plum tomatoes, seeded and diced
1½	cups peeled, diced ripe mango
½	cup diced onion
½	cup chopped fresh cilantro
2	tbsp. fresh lime juice
1	tbsp. cider vinegar
1	tsp. sugar
1	tsp. salt, divided
1	tsp. black pepper, divided
2	cloves garlic, minced
4	(6-oz.) halibut fillets
1	tbsp. olive oil
1	tsp. cayenne

PREP

1. To make the salsa, combine first seven ingredients and stir in 1/2 tsp. salt, 1/2 tsp. pepper and garlic.

2. Rub halibut with oil and dust with 1/2 tsp. salt and 1/2 tsp. pepper. Place fish on grill rack and grill 3 minutes on each side or until fish flakes with a fork.

3. Serve with mango salsa. There's nothing wrong with making a double batch of the salsa and serving it up with some chips—people are gonna want more.

DID YOU KNOW?

The mango is a major Peruvian export. Another dynamite export from Peru? Duke's wife, Pilar. He met her in Peru in 1953, while scouting locations for *The Alamo*.

UPSCALE SCALLOPS
WITH TOMATO SAUCE AND SHORT PASTA

Scallops are high in protein and class, and they rate high on the flavor scale as well. This refreshing, easy-to-make dish tastes especially great at the height of summer when tomatoes are at their peak.

PROVISIONS

- 1 large tomato, seeded and chopped
- ½ cup chopped green onions
- 1 (⅔-oz.) package fresh mint leaves, chopped
- ⅓ cup orange juice
- ⅓ cup olive oil
- ¼ tsp. salt
- ¼ tsp. freshly ground black pepper
- 3 lb. sea scallops
- 2 cups hot cooked orzo (short pasta)
- Salt and pepper to taste

PREP

1. Combine first seven ingredients in a bowl. Cover and chill for 2 hours.

2. Drain and reserve juice from the tomato mixture; set mixture and juice aside.

3. Thread scallops evenly onto skewers. Shake on salt and pepper, then brush scallops with the rest of the juice.

4. Grill scallops with lid on over medium-high heat for 3 to 4 minutes on each side or until scallops are opaque.

5. Serve over cooked orzo and top with the tomato sauce.

WAYNE FAMILY TIP

If you're using wood skewers for this or any dish, soak them in water for about 20 minutes beforehand to keep the ends from catching fire while you grill them.

JAMAICAN-STYLE SWORDFISH STEAKS

Jamaican dishes are influenced by the cuisine of many cultures, including Mexican, West Indian and African. A unique blend of seasonings make these swordfish steaks anything but ordinary.

PROVISIONS

- ¾ cup plain yogurt
- 1 tbsp. Jamaican jerk seasoning
- 1 tbsp. fresh lemon juice
- 1 tsp. garlic powder
- 1 tsp. ground cumin
- 1 tsp. chili powder
- ½ tsp. ground cinnamon
- ½ tsp. ground ginger
- 4 (6-oz.) swordfish steaks (about ¾-inch thick)

PREP

1. Combine the first eight ingredients in a large bowl. Add fish, flipping to coat. Cover and refrigerate for 1 hour, flipping the bag occasionally.

2. Prepare grill.

3. Place fish on grill rack coated with olive oil; grill for 4 minutes on each side or until fish flakes easily when tested with a fork or to desired degree of doneness.

DID YOU KNOW?

Duke loved sport fishing in the Gulf of California. The 68,340-square-mile span between Mexico and the Baja California Peninsula is a swordfish haven.

FRESH TROUT FILLETS
TOPPED WITH CITRUS CRUNCH

Rainbow trout is one of the most sustainably raised fish, and they thrive in the wild west of the Rockies. Because it's dense and oily, the fish is less likely to stick to the grill than others, so after you eat, it's easier to clean your setup.

WAYNE FAMILY TIP

To keep delicate pieces of trout from breaking apart on your spatula, grill it on a bed of lemon slices. It'll add a zip of flavor and will keep you from cursing at your dinner when it crumbles into your charcoal.

PROVISIONS

- 2 tbsp. pine nuts
- ¼ cup extra-virgin olive oil, divided
- ½ cup panko crumbs (Japanese bread crumbs)
- 2 oil-packed anchovy fillets, minced
- 1 tbsp. minced garlic (3 medium cloves)
- ¾ tsp. salt, divided
- 2 tsp. very finely shredded lemon zest
- 1 tbsp. finely chopped flat-leaf parsley leaves
- 2 medium heads radicchio
- 4 (½-inch thick) skin-on trout fillets
- 1 tbsp. lemon juice
- Freshly ground black pepper

PREP

1. Toast pine nuts in a wide (not nonstick) frying pan over medium heat until lightly toasted or about 3 minutes. Pour into a medium bowl and set to the side.

2. In the same pan, heat 1 tbsp. olive oil over medium heat until it's warm, then add panko. Toast the panko, stirring occasionally, for about 5 minutes or until it darkens up. Add the anchovies and garlic; stir to combine well.

3. Add the panko mixture to pine nuts. Stir in 1/4 tsp. salt, lemon zest and parsley and set aside.

4. Preheat grill. Cut each radicchio head in half, then cut each half into thirds; brush cut sides with olive oil. Place wedges onto metal skewers, three per skewer. Grill the radicchio (close the lid if you're cooking over gas) for 2 minutes, then turn skewers to grill opposite side for about 2 minutes. Remove radicchio from skewers and chop roughly. Toss with remaining lemon juice and 1/2 tsp. salt.

5. Brush fish on both sides with olive oil and grill, skin side down, for 3 to 4 minutes (close that lid again, gas grillers) or until fillets look opaque. Using two spatulas, gently turn fish over and cook for 1 minute. Carefully remove from the grill and transfer the fillets to plates.

6. Stir remaining 3 tbsp. olive oil into panko mixture and spoon over the flesh side of fish. Season with salt, pepper and a few drops of lemon juice to taste. Serve with a side of grilled radicchio.

GRILLED WILD SALMON

WITH MUSHROOM SAUCE AND ROASTED BEETS

Great Alaskan Wild

Although John Wayne's 1960 film North to Alaska *is set in the 49th state, most of it was filmed in California—the cabin is near a creek later used in* True Grit *(1969). Alaska is a major source of wild salmon, and more than half the nation's seafood is harvested there.*

The savory mushroom sauce matched with the rustic flavor of beets kick this salmon dish up a notch. If you're feeling fancy, feel free to serve the entire meal over a bed of arugula.

PROVISIONS

SALMON

18	baby red beets
18	baby yellow beets
	Olive oil
1	lb. wild Pacific salmon
	Salt
	Freshly ground black pepper
½	lb. arugula (optional)

SAUCE

3	cups chicken broth
2	tbsp. chopped dried porcini or shiitake mushrooms
2	tsp. chopped fresh rosemary
1	large garlic clove, chopped
⅓	cup balsamic vinegar
1	tbsp. butter
	Salt
	Freshly ground black pepper

PREP

1. To make the sauce, put the first four ingredients in a saucepan over high heat and bring to a boil. Cook over high heat for 15 to 20 minutes or until reduced by half. Stir in vinegar. Cook for 10 minutes or until mixture has reduced to about 1/2 cup and has the consistency of a light sauce.

2. Remove from heat, strain sauce through a fine-mesh strainer and return to pan. Whisk in butter. Season to taste with salt and pepper.

3. To cook beets, scrub them thoroughly and remove greens. Drizzle lightly with olive oil and place in a roasting pan. Bake, covered with foil, at 400° for 30 minutes or until tender. Rub the skins off beets with a towel and slice.

4. For salmon, remove any bones, then brush with olive oil and season lightly with salt and pepper. Grill salmon over medium-hot coals on both sides until medium rare (translucent in the center). Spread some sauce on the plates and top with beet slices. Cut salmon into servings and place on plates or on a bed of greens.

GRILLED SHRIMP
WITH TARATOR SAUCE

Let's face it: Shrimp are great whether they're boiled, fried or grilled. But grilling them adds a rich flavor you won't get through other cooking methods and is about as simple as tying your shoes. The toughest thing about this dish is the tarator sauce, which you'll find worth the effort as it cools things down on even the hottest summer day.

WAYNE FAMILY TIP

When you're grilling small items like shrimp, use two skewers to prevent the pieces from rotating or falling off into the grill.

PROVISIONS

SHRIMP

2¾	lb. (about 50) fresh large shrimp, peeled and deveined
½	cup extra virgin olive oil
2	large garlic cloves, thinly sliced
4	fresh rosemary sprigs

SAUCE

2	cups pine nuts
3	slices firm-textured white bread with crust removed, torn into 1-inch pieces
½	cup fresh lemon juice
2	cloves garlic
¾	tsp. salt
½	tsp. freshly ground pepper

PREP

1. Place sauce ingredients in a food processor with 1/3 cup water and process for 30 seconds. Scrape sides of bowl and process 30 more seconds or until smooth. Cover and chill until ready to serve.

2. Place first three shrimp ingredients in a large shallow baking dish and toss well. Squeeze the rosemary sprigs to release flavor, then add to shrimp mixture. Cover and refrigerate for 3 to 4 hours.

3. Thread 5 shrimp on each of the 10 long skewers, leaving space between shrimp. Grill with lid on over high heat for 1 1/2 minutes on each side or to desired degree of doneness.

4. Serve hot or at room temperature with tarator sauce.

Fishing was one of Duke's favorite ways to pass time.

SOUTHWEST GROUPER SANDWICH
WITH CHIPOTLE TARTAR SAUCE

Chipotle-flavored tartar sauce is a smoky variation on a classic, perfect for anything from grouper to French fries to crab cakes. A dash of chipotle pepper adds full, rich flavor.

PROVISIONS

- ¾ cup mayonnaise
- 2 tbsp. diced celery
- 1 tbsp. minced onion
- 2 tbsp. dill pickle relish
- 1 tbsp. canned chipotle peppers in adobo sauce, minced
- 4 (5-oz.) grouper fillets
- 4 tsp. lemon pepper
- 4 Kaiser rolls, toasted on grill
- 1 tomato, sliced
- 1 red onion, sliced
- 4 Napa cabbage leaves

PREP

1. To make chipotle tartar sauce, combine first five ingredients in a small bowl. Cover and stick in the fridge for 3 hours.

2. Dust grouper with lemon pepper. Grill your fillets with the lid on over medium-high heat for 4 minutes on each side·or until fish flakes with a fork.

3. Place each fillet on a Kaiser roll. Top with chipotle tartar sauce, tomato, onion and cabbage.

FISH

WAYNE FAMILY TIP

If you want fresh fish but aren't able to catch them yourself, try buying them whole from your local market. You can look a fish in the eyes to determine its quality. The clearer the eye, the fresher the catch.

**PLAIN AND SIMPLE
PORK TENDERLOIN**
PAGE 162

PORK

One of the most versatile meats, whether it's sliced into bacon or shredded into barbecue, pork is practically its own food group.

Honey-Mustard Pork Tenderloin

Fall-off-the-Bone Baby Back Ribs

Asian Grilled Pork

Jerk-style Ribs with Sticky Rum BBQ Sauce

Plain and Simple Pork Tenderloin

Spicy Pork Skewers

World's Greatest Grilled Pork Roast

Knock-out Pork Chops with Shallot Butter

Pork Tacos with Summer Salsa

Red River Ribs

Spiced Pork Patties with Spring Greens

Mustard-Molasses Pork Chops

Beer-Soaked Spicy Ribs

Pork Chops with Herb Butter

Apricot Pork Chops

HONEY-MUSTARD PORK TENDERLOIN

This succulent pork tenderloin is marinated in a delicious honey-mustard sauce, a Carolina pairing fit for eating anywhere in the country.

PROVISIONS

- 2½ lb. pork tenderloin
- ½ cup chopped fresh parsley
- ½ cup red wine vinegar
- ¼ cup olive oil
- ¼ cup honey
- 3 tbsp. country-Dijon mustard
- 2 cloves garlic, minced
- 1 tbsp. kosher salt
- 1½ tsp. coarsely ground pepper

PREP

1. Remove silver skin from tenderloin, leaving a thin layer of fat covering the tenderloin.

2. Stir together chopped parsley and the next 7 ingredients until blended. Pour mixture in a large, shallow dish or zip-top plastic bag; add pork, cover or seal and chill for at least 2 hours and up to 8 hours, flipping occasionally. Remove pork, discarding marinade.

3. Heat grill to medium-high. Grill tenderloin with grill lid closed for 8 to 10 minutes, flipping once. Let rest for 10 minutes, then slice and serve.

FALL-OFF-THE-BONE BABY BACK RIBS

For super-tender meat, marinate baby back ribs in beer and bake in the oven for three hours before grilling. These ribs grill for just 10 to 15 minutes because they will have been almost cooked through in the oven.

PROVISIONS

1	large onion, sliced
3½	lb. (about 2 slabs) baby back ribs
1	(12-oz.) bottle beer
	Salt and pepper
2	cups of your favorite barbeque sauce

PREP

1. Preheat oven to 350°. Spread onion slices evenly on a rimmed baking sheet and place ribs, bone side down, on top. Pour beer over ribs, sprinkle with salt and pepper and cover with foil. Bake for 3 hours.

2. Brush both sides of ribs with barbeque sauce. Grill over medium heat, meat side down, for 10 to 15 minutes or until slightly charred and crispy, basting several times with sauce. Flip ribs over and baste cooked side liberally. Close grill lid and cook 10 to 15 minutes more, basting often. Remove from heat; let rest for 10 minutes. Cut individual ribs apart and serve warm.

DID YOU KNOW?

Although Duke won an Oscar for his role as Rooster Cogburn in *True Grit* (1969), he earned his first nomination 20 years earlier for his performance in *Sands of Iwo Jima* (1949).

Duke as Sgt. John M. Stryker in *Sands of Iwo Jima* (1949).

JOHN WAYNE

37 USA

2004

ASIAN GRILLED PORK

Marinate center-cut pork chops in a mixture of soy sauce, honey, lime juice and ginger to get a quick and easy Asian flavor. The marinade serves a dual purpose: In addition to the stellar flavor, it'll tenderize the pork even further, making for a tasty and tender meal.

PROVISIONS

- **1** tbsp. soy sauce
- **1** tbsp. vegetable oil
- **½** tbsp. honey
- **½** tbsp. fresh lime juice
- **½** tsp. powdered ginger
- **1** large clove garlic, smashed
- **8** thin, center-cut pork chops (about 1¾ lb.)
- **2** scallions, chopped

PREP

1. Combine soy sauce, oil, honey, lime juice, ginger and garlic in a large zip-top bag. Add pork chops, squeeze out air, seal and flip to coat pork. Stick in the fridge for 15 minutes.

2. Prepare a grill or grease a grill pan and place over medium heat. When hot, add chops and cook until nicely marked and just cooked through, about 7 minutes total, flipping once. Transfer chops to a platter and let stand for 3 minutes before serving. Top with scallions.

JERK-STYLE RIBS
WITH STICKY RUM BBQ SAUCE

Get a taste of the islands by topping your baby back ribs with spicy jerk seasoning, marinating them in rum, then basting them with a tangy brown sugar and rum sauce.

PROVISIONS

SAUCE

- 1 cup firmly packed dark or light brown sugar
- ½ cup ketchup
- ½ cup dark rum
- 1 tbsp. jerk seasoning blend
- 1 tsp. lime zest
- 2 tbsp. fresh lime juice
- 2 tbsp. soy sauce
- 1 tsp. grated fresh ginger
- 2 cloves garlic, minced

RIBS

- 2 (2-lb.) racks baby back pork ribs
- 1 tbsp. jerk seasoning blend
- 1 cup dark or spiced rum

PREP

1. For sauce, combine all ingredients in a saucepan over medium heat. Simmer for 5 to 7 minutes or until slightly thickened. Remove from heat and let sauce cool; refrigerate, covered, for up to 2 weeks.

2. Rinse and pat ribs dry. Rub ribs evenly with jerk seasoning.

3. Pour rum in zip-top plastic bag and add ribs, turning to coat. Seal and refrigerate for 1 hour, flipping every so often.

4. Light one side of grill, heating to medium. Place a drip pan beneath unlit side. Remove ribs from marinade, let drain quickly and place on grate above drip pan. Grill with lid closed, flipping occasionally, for 2 1/2 to 3 hours or until ribs are browned and tender and meat has shrunk back from bones.

DID YOU KNOW?

Rum's got nothing on John Wayne. To date, the priciest case of the spirit sold for $128,000; the beret John Wayne wore in *The Green Berets* sold for $179,250.

PLAIN AND SIMPLE PORK TENDERLOIN

The best part about pork tenderloin is slicing the finished product. And eating it, obviously. Cut hearty hunks for your hungriest guests and smaller slices for the less interested. Slicing at a 45-degree angle will allow you to get a few more pieces out of one loin.

PROVISIONS

- 1 tbsp. ground cumin
- 1 tsp. cracked black pepper
- 2 tbsp. smoked paprika
- 2 cloves garlic, minced
- 2 (1-lb.) pork tenderloins
- ½ tsp. salt
- 2 rosemary sprigs

PREP

1. Mix first 4 ingredients together in a small bowl, until they well-blended. Massage onto the outside of each pork loin until both are well covered. Double your spice mixture if necessary.

2. Cover and stick in the fridge for up to 8 hours.

3. Top pork with salt and grill, covered, over medium-high heat. While grilling, flip each loin every 5 minutes for 18 to 20 minutes or until thermometer registers 155° and the tenderloins are slightly pink in center. For extra flavor, drag a rosemary sprig over the pork each time you flip it.

4. Place pork on a cutting board, loosely cover with foil and let stand for 10 minutes, rosemary sprigs on top, before slicing.

SPICY PORK SKEWERS

If dinner needs to be done in a hurry, break out this simple, no-nonsense pork dish. You'll be good to go just a few minutes after the grill's fired up.

PROVISIONS

- 1¼ lb. ground pork
- 1½ tbsp. minced garlic
- 2 tsp. ground cumin
- 2 tsp. ground paprika
- ⅓ cup finely chopped onion
- 1½ tsp. salt
- 1 tsp. freshly ground black pepper

PREP

1. In a medium bowl, stir together the pork, garlic, cumin, paprika, onion, salt and pepper. Form into meatballs, each about the size of a golf ball, then thread the meat onto the skewers.

2. Lay skewers over medium coals. (If you are cooking with gas, close the lid.) Cook, turning once, for about 8 minutes or until browned on both sides and no longer pink in the center. Serve warm.

DID YOU KNOW?

After Duke first kisses Maureen O'Hara in *The Quiet Man*, she slaps him. O'Hara broke her hand in the process but was unable to wear a cast until the movie was wrapped.

PORK

WORLD'S GREATEST GRILLED PORK ROAST

While some would argue that burgers and apple pie are the most American grub there is, they'll both find a worthy adversary for the title in a classic pork roast. Use this simple rub to give your already-delicious pork a kick, then slow grill it for mouthwatering results.

PROVISIONS

2   cloves garlic, minced

1½ tsp. onion powder

1   tsp. salt

1   tsp. pepper

2   tsp. poultry seasoning

1   tsp. chili powder

1   (3-lb.) boneless center-cut pork loin roast

PREP

1. Prepare your grill for indirect-heat cooking. You may also want to use your cast-iron skillet to catch the drippings from your roast, which you can later serve with it once you're finished cooking.

2. Mix the first six ingredients and massage the rub onto your pork roast.

3. Place roast on grill, fat side up. Cover grill and cook for 1 hour, 40 minutes to 2 hours, 10 minutes or until thickest part of roast registers 160° on a meat thermometer. Wait 15 minutes and slice.

Secret Weapon

You can use the recipe here to make a quick and easy rub for a pork roast. But if you want maximum results your neighbors will be talking about for days, reach for John Wayne Pork Rub from Fire and Flavor. Much like Duke, it's a bold classic you won't forget.

JOHN WAYNE
★ALL NATURAL★
PORK
SPICE RUB

NET WT 2.7oz (76.5g)

John Wayne as
Stony Brooke in *Red
River Range* (1938).

KNOCK-OUT PORK CHOPS
WITH SHALLOT BUTTER

A savory shallot spread adds the right amount of pop to these chops. If made ahead, let your butter come to room temperature before spreading it over the pork. You can also combine your oil and herbs a few hours in advance.

PROVISIONS

8	(7-oz.) bone-in center-cut pork chops
1	tsp. salt, divided
¾	tsp. freshly ground black pepper
2	tbsp. extra virgin olive oil
2	tbsp. finely chopped fresh chives
1	tbsp. finely chopped fresh thyme
1	tsp. finely chopped fresh rosemary
3	cloves garlic, minced
2	tbsp. butter, softened
2½	tsp. minced shallots
¼	tsp. grated lemon rind

PREP

1. Prepare grill to medium-high heat.

2. Sprinkle both sides of pork evenly with 1/2 tsp. salt and pepper. Combine oil, chives, thyme, rosemary and garlic, stirring well. Rub oil mixture evenly over both sides of pork. Place pork on grill rack and grill for 6 minutes on each side. Remove pork from grill and let stand for 5 minutes. Sprinkle with remaining 1/2 tsp. salt.

3. Combine butter, shallots and lemon rind, stirring well. Spread about 1 tsp. butter mixture over each pork chop; let the pork stand for an additional 5 minutes, then serve.

WAYNE FAMILY TIP

Throw two or three quartered onions onto your charcoal before you start grilling to infuse your meat with a little bit of extra flavor.

PORK TACOS
WITH SUMMER SALSA

These grilled pork tacos are the perfect mix of flavor and presentation that'll have your friends thinking you went to some fancy cooking college.

PROVISIONS

- 2 **tbsp. fresh lime juice, divided**
- 1½ **tbsp. extra virgin olive oil, divided**
- 4 **(4-oz.) boneless center-cut loin pork chops**
- ¾ **tsp. salt, divided**
- ½ **tsp. ground cumin**
- ¼ **tsp. freshly ground black pepper**
- 1 **clove garlic, minced**
- 1 **ear shucked corn**
- ¼ **cup diced red bell pepper**
- ½ **cup diced ripe nectarine**
- ½ **tsp. grated lime rind**
- 1 **seeded jalapeño pepper, minced**
- 8 **(6-inch) corn tortillas**
- 1 **cup shredded cabbage**

PREP

1. Heat grill to medium-high heat.

2. Combine 2 tsp. lime juice, 1 tbsp. oil and pork in a zip-top plastic bag and seal. Marinate for 10 minutes at room temperature. Remove pork from bag and discard marinade. Sprinkle both sides of pork with 1/2 tsp. salt, cumin, pepper and garlic. Put pork on a greased grill rack and grill for 3 minutes on each side or to desired degree of doneness. Let stand for 5 minutes. Slice pork into strips.

3. Lightly coat corn with cooking spray. Place corn on a lightly greased grill rack and grill for 6 minutes or until lightly charred, turning occasionally. Let corn stand for 5 minutes; cut kernels from cob. Combine kernels, 2 tsp. juice, remaining 1 1/2 tsp. oil, remaining 1/4 tsp. salt, bell pepper and next 3 ingredients (through jalapeño) in a bowl and toss to make salsa.

4. Put tortillas on a lightly greased grill rack and grill for 1 minute on each side or until lightly browned. Toss cabbage with remaining 2 tsp. lime juice. Place 2 tortillas on each of 4 plates and divide pork among tortillas. Top each taco with about 1 tbsp. cabbage mixture and about 2 tbsp. salsa.

Two Big Stars

Duke preferred to act alongside men who were as tall as he was, which is why he suggested the 6'4" Rock Hudson for the role of Col. James Langdon in the Mexico-based epic The Undefeated (1969).

PORK

RED RIVER RIBS

This recipe is handy for entertaining because the initial cooking can be done up to a day ahead. The ribs can then be quickly finished on the grill or in the oven just before serving.

PROVISIONS

SAUCE

2	cups brown sugar
1	cup hot sauce
2	cups cider vinegar
½	cup molasses

RIBS

2½	lb. (about 2 racks) St. Louis-style ribs
½	cup olive oil
	Sea salt
	Freshly ground pepper

PREP

1. For sauce, combine ingredients in a heavy nonstick saucepan and bring to a boil. Reduce heat to low, and simmer for about an hour. Sauce should be thick and shiny. Refrigerate.

2. Preheat oven to 350°. Drizzle both sides of ribs with oil and sprinkle with salt and pepper to taste. Place on baking rack over rimmed baking sheet. Add 1 1/2 cups water to baking sheet and cover tightly with foil. Roast for 3 hours or until ribs are tender. Meat should separate easily from bone.

3. Remove ribs from oven and let rest for at least 20 minutes.

4. Brush ribs on both sides with sauce and grill over medium heat for 5 to 6 minutes per side.

SPICED PORK PATTIES
WITH SPRING GREENS

They might not win a beauty contest, but what these pork patties lack in looks they make up for in flavor and simplicity. Serve over a basic salad or split a few kaiser rolls to make sandwiches perfect for a backyard cookout.

PROVISIONS

1	lb. ground pork
1	tsp. ground coriander
1	tsp. cumin
½	tsp. cinnamon
¼	tsp. nutmeg
1	large egg, beaten
½	onion, finely chopped
¼	cup finely chopped fresh parsley
2	cloves garlic, chopped and divided
1	tsp. salt
1	cup plain whole-milk yogurt
1½	tsp. lemon juice
10	cups mixed salad greens
1	cup shredded cabbage

PREP

1. Heat grill to medium. In bowl, combine pork, coriander, cumin, cinnamon, nutmeg, egg, onion, parsley, 1 garlic clove and 1 tsp. salt. Mix thoroughly with your hands. Form mixture into 1 1/2-inch balls, then press into football shapes.

2. Grease up your grill grates. Grill patties, turning once, until cooked through or 8 to 10 minutes total.

3. In a small bowl, combine yogurt, lemon juice, 1/2 tsp. salt and remaining garlic. Divide salad greens among 4 serving plates. Top with patties and drizzle with yogurt sauce. Serve immediately.

MUSTARD-MOLASSES PORK CHOPS

Served with a garlicky sauce composed of balsamic vinegar, molasses, mustard and fresh rosemary, then finished with a little crumbled Gorgonzola, these pork chops hit the spot no matter the weather.

PROVISIONS

- ⅔ cup balsamic vinegar
- ⅔ cup molasses
- 2 large cloves garlic, minced (about 1 tbsp.)
- 1½ tbsp. finely chopped fresh rosemary
- ½ cup Dijon mustard, divided
- 8 (¾-inch-thick) bone-in pork loin chops (about 4 lb. total)
- 2 tbsp. olive oil
- 1 tsp. salt
- 1 tsp. pepper
- 1 tbsp. butter
- 4 oz. crumbled Gorgonzola (about 1 cup)

PREP

1. Whisk vinegar, molasses, garlic, rosemary and 1/4 cup mustard in a bowl. Divide marinade between 2 large zip-lock bags and add chops, flipping to coat. Seal and chill for 2 hours, flipping occasionally.

2. Heat grill to medium-high. Remove chops from marinade, shaking off excess. Set aside marinade. Brush chops with oil; sprinkle with salt and pepper.

3. Grill chops, covered, for 5 to 6 minutes on each side. Transfer chops to a plate and cover loosely with foil; let stand.

4. Whisk set-aside marinade and remaining 1/4 cup mustard in a small saucepan. Bring to a boil over medium-high heat and cook, stirring frequently, for 4 minutes. (Sauce will be thick.) Remove from heat and whisk in butter until melted. Spoon sauce over chops, sprinkle with Gorgonzola and serve.

WAYNE FAMILY TIP

Plan ahead. Meat tastes best when left in its marinade overnight and put on the grill at room temperature. For flavor and simplicity's sake, do your prep the day before you grill out.

BEER-SOAKED SPICY RIBS

This rib dish takes a fair amount of planning, but all of the thinking ahead will pay off. Marinate your ribs two days ahead, grill them the day before, then reheat them on your grill at the party when you're ready to eat.

PROVISIONS

- ¾ cup harissa paste
- 3 tbsp. fresh lemon juice
- 1 tbsp. minced garlic
- 2 (1½-lb.) slabs baby back ribs
- Kosher salt and freshly ground black pepper
- 2 (12-oz.) bottles beer, any type

PREP

1. In a small bowl, stir together harissa, lemon juice and garlic. Set aside.

2. Rinse ribs and pat dry. Use a dull butter knife to loosen the thin papery membrane that runs along underside, then pull it off with your fingers. Rub ribs generously on both sides with salt and pepper, then slather with homemade harissa rub. Wrap ribs in plastic wrap and marinate, refrigerated, for at least 8 and up to 24 hours.

3. Set up grill for medium indirect heat. Place ribs, bone side down, on the cooler part of the grill and close the lid. Cook, basting with beer on both sides every 10 minutes (keep ribs bone side down), for 40 to 50 minutes or until ribs are tender and cooked through and meat has shrunk back from ends of the bones. Try to keep harissa paste on the ribs while basting. Serve ribs hot.

True Grit

While filming the 1969 epic The Undefeated, John Wayne fell off his horse and fractured three ribs. After only two weeks of bed rest he was back in the saddle, fighting through immense pain to keep the film on track.

John Wayne sits with director and friend John Ford on the set of *The Horse Soldiers* (1959).

PORK CHOPS
WITH HERB BUTTER

John Wayne wasn't much for complicating things. In that spirit, these chops are basic but far from boring. With a handful of ingredients, you'll dish out an endless amount of flavor.

PROVISIONS

- 4 tbsp. butter, softened
- 1 tbsp. finely chopped fresh chives
- 1 tbsp. finely chopped fresh parsley
- ½ tsp. Dijon mustard
- 4 (2-lb.) bone-in center-cut pork chops
- Salt and pepper

PREP

1. Mash butter, chives, parsley and mustard in a bowl with a fork until smooth. Cover with plastic wrap and let stand at cool room temperature.

2. Heat grill to high. After 10 minutes, lower heat to medium. Pat pork chops dry with paper towels and sprinkle generously with salt and pepper. Grill, turning once, for 12 to 14 minutes total. Transfer chops to a platter and top each with 1 tbsp. herb butter. Tent with foil to keep warm, let stand for 5 minutes and then serve hot.

PORK

Pappy and Duke

Duke and legendary director John Ford, or "Coach" as Duke called him, collaborated on more than 20 films. Their friendship lasted until Ford's death in 1973. Duke eulogized Ford at the funeral.

John Wayne enjoys some time on set with his youngest son, Ethan.

APRICOT PORK CHOPS

The beauty of pork chops is they're easy to make. The danger, of course, is overcooking them. Avoid making pork jerky on your grill by glazing these chops with an apricot sauce and keeping an eye on the heat and cook time.

PROVISIONS

⅔   **cup white wine**

⅓   **cup apricot preserves**

1   **tsp. finely chopped fresh thyme leaves**

    Salt

4   **bone-in center-cut pork chops (about 3 lb.)**

1   **tbsp. vegetable oil**

PREP

1. In a pot, mix wine, preserves, thyme and 1/2 tsp. salt. Bring to a boil over medium-high heat and cook until reduced by half. Cool.

2. Heat grill to medium-high. Rub chops with oil and sprinkle with salt. Grill for 10 minutes, turning once. Continue to cook, basting with glaze several times, 6 to 8 minutes longer. Let chops rest on a cutting board for 5 minutes before serving.

DID YOU KNOW?

California produces the most apricots of any state in America. Duke was a longtime—and easily recognizable—resident of the Golden State. "People might call out 'Hey Duke!' when he was running errands," Ethan says.

BURGER
PAGE 194

BURGERS & DOGS

Whether you're cooking for your family or a family reunion, burgers and dogs are fast, flavorful and almost universally beloved.

All-American Burger

Tennessee Burger with Bourbon and BBQ Sauce

Big Game Ham- and Swiss-Stuffed Burgers

Great Plains Burger

New England Turkey Burger

Beer-Basted Sausages

Western Sausage 'n' Veggie Kebabs

Hot Dog How-To

Confetti Corn Dog

California Pup Dog

Hawaiian Dog

Cookout Cruncher Dog

ALL-AMERICAN BURGER

Even though it's got a funny German name, the only thing more American than John Wayne himself might be the good old-fashioned hamburger. Make perfect patties every time with this classic recipe and these essential tips.

PROVISIONS

- 1½ lb. fresh ground chuck
- 1 tsp. salt

PREP

1. In a large bowl, pull the meat apart into small chunks, add salt and toss gently with fingers spread apart until loosely mixed. Mix salt into your meat very gently—the more you handle the meat, the tougher your burger will be.

2. Use wet hands to form patties. This keeps your hands from getting sticky and also allows the meat to come together faster, preventing overhandling. You can also rub a little olive oil between your palms to add flavor while cutting down on stick.

3. Divide the meat into four equal portions and form patties about 3/4-inch thick at the edges and 1/2-inch thick at the center. Don't worry—the patties will shrink and even out during cooking.

4. Keep patties cold until they go on the grill. This helps more of the flavor-carrying fat stay in the meat.

5. Use a clean, well-greased, preheated grill. Bits of debris encourage sticking, as does an unoiled surface or a temperature that's too low. You want your burgers to sizzle quickly, firm up and release from the grill.

6. Keep grill at a steady high heat so you can hold your hand 1 to 2 inches above grill level for only 2 to 3 seconds. If using charcoal, go with ash-covered coals to produce even heat. If using a gas grill, keep the lid down while cooking; with a charcoal grill, leave the lid up.

7. Flip burgers once, at the right time. Constant turning will toughen and dry out meat; flip too soon and burgers will stick. Cook 2 minutes per side for rare, 3 for medium-rare, 4 for medium and 5 for well done.

8. Don't press the burgers while they're cooking. The juice that escapes holds most of the flavor and moisture. You want that juice in your mouth, not on your coals.

9. Let burgers rest a few minutes before eating to allow them to finish cooking. This also allows their juices, which have collected on the surface during grilling, to redistribute throughout the patty.

OPTIONAL

If you like a charred burger that's juicy on the inside, mold your patties with a single ice cube inside. This leaves the inside of your burgers nice and tasty, while the outside develops a crispy char.

WAYNE FAMILY TIPS

Getting the most out of your burgers, brats and dogs.

The right amount of fat is important to a burger's taste. When picking beef, buy meat that's about 80 percent lean and 20 percent fat.

Burgers can't be too rich. Whether you add some mayonnaise or an egg yolk while forming your patties, the extra moisture will only improve your burgers' flavor.

Toasting your buns puts dogs and burgers over the top. Set them on the grill for a minute or two and rejoice in making the right decision.

Cooking dogs over high heat is a recipe for a charred meal. Use medium heat to avoid burnt, shrivelled franks that still have icy insides.

When cooking sausages, pull them from the grill before the casing starts to burst so the tasty juices don't escape.

TENNESSEE BURGER
WITH BOURBON AND BBQ SAUCE

This burger is a Southern triple threat, loaded with some of the best things in life: bacon, BBQ sauce and bourbon—three staples Duke always agreed with.

PROVISIONS

- 3   bacon slices
- 1   tsp. extra virgin olive oil
- 3   cups red onion, vertically sliced
- 5   tbsp. bourbon, divided
- 1   tbsp. balsamic vinegar
- ½   tsp. kosher salt, divided
- ½   cup ketchup
- 1   tbsp. Dijon mustard
- 2   tsp. honey
- 2   tsp. hot pepper sauce
- 2   tsp. Worcestershire sauce
- ¼   tsp. smoked paprika
- ¼   tsp. garlic powder
- ¼   tsp. onion powder
- 1½   lb. 90% lean ground sirloin
- 6   (1½-oz.) French bread hamburger buns
- 6   (¼-inch-thick) slices of tomato

PREP

1. Cook bacon in a large skillet over medium heat until it's crisp. Remove bacon from pan. Add oil and onion to drippings in pan; cook for 15 minutes or until onion is brown and tender, stirring every so often. Add 3 tbsp. bourbon, vinegar and 1/4 tsp. salt. Cook for 2 minutes or until liquid almost evaporates, stirring occasionally. Remove mixture from pan and cool for 5 minutes.

2. Combine left over 2 tbsp. bourbon, ketchup and next seven ingredients in a small saucepan. Bring to a boil, stirring often. Reduce heat and simmer for 5 minutes or until sauce thickens. Remove from heat.

3. Heat grill to medium-high. Coarsely chop 3/4 cup onion mixture and stir into beef. Divide beef mixture into six equal portions, shaping each one into a 1/2-inch-thick patty. Press a thumb-sized indentation in center of each patty. Sprinkle evenly with remaining 1/4 tsp. salt. Put the patties on a well-greased grill grate and grill for about 4 minutes on each side or to desired degree of doneness.

4. Spread each bun half with 1 tbsp. sauce. Put patties on bottom halves and top each patty with one tomato slice. Divide remaining onion mixture evenly among burgers and top each with 1/2 bacon slice and top half of bun.

BIG GAME HAM- AND SWISS-STUFFED BURGERS

When you need a big meal before the big game, the only thing better than meat is more meat. This ham- and swiss-stuffed burger is a tasty alternative to the classic patty, and it's just as simple to make.

PROVISIONS

- 1   tbsp. dried parsley
- 1   tbsp. Worcestershire sauce
- ¼   tsp. salt
- ¼   tsp. garlic powder
- ¼   tsp. freshly ground black pepper
- 1   lb. ground round
- ½   cup (2 oz.) shredded Swiss cheese
- 2   oz. smoked deli ham, thinly sliced
- 8   (1-oz.) slices sourdough bread
- 4   curly leaf lettuce leaves
- 8   (¼-inch-thick) slices red onion
- 8   (¼-inch-thick) slices tomato

PREP

1. Prepare grill, setting it to high heat and greasing its grates.

2. Combine first six ingredients. Divide mixture into eight equal portions, forming each into a 5-inch oval patty. These are going to be the tops and bottoms of your burgers. Take four of the patties and top them with 2 tbsp. cheese and 1/2 oz. ham, leaving a 1/2-inch border around the outer edges; top with remaining patties. Press edges together to seal.

3. Put patties on your grill rack. Grill for 3 minutes on each side or until done. Place bread on grill rack and grill for 1 minute on each side or until toasted. Top each of four bread slices with one lettuce leaf, two onion slices, one patty, two tomato slices and one bread slice.

GREAT PLAINS BURGER

John Wayne's roots lie in the corn capital of our country: Iowa. Corn is a staple in this recipe, from creamy corn mayo to corn chips in the patties.

PROVISIONS

1	shucked ear corn
1	small red onion, cut into ¾-inch slices
2	tbsp. mayonnaise
1	tsp. mustard seeds
1	tsp. cider vinegar
⅜	tsp. salt, divided
1	tbsp. adobo sauce from canned chipotle chiles in adobo sauce
1½	oz. corn chips
1	tbsp. chopped fresh sage
½	tsp. garlic powder
½	tsp. freshly ground black pepper
1	lb. lean ground bison
4	(1½-oz.) onion rolls, toasted

PREP

1. Heat grill to high. Throw corn and onion on a well-greased grill rack. Grill for 9 minutes or until charred. Don't forget to flip your corn every so often and turn your onion once.

2. When you're done cooking, cut kernels from the ear. Combine corn, mayonnaise, mustard seeds, vinegar and 1/8 tsp. salt in a mini food processor; process until smooth. Combine onion and adobo sauce.

3. Put corn chips in a food processor and pulse until coarsely chopped. Smashing them yourself works, too. Mix chips, 1/4 tsp. salt, sage, garlic powder, pepper and bison. Divide mixture into four equal portions, shaping each into a 1/2-inch-thick patty. Make a thumb-shaped indentation in center of each patty.

4. Put your patties on a well-greased grill rack and grill for 3 minutes. Flip patties and grill for 3 minutes or to desired degree of doneness.

5 Place one patty on bottom half of each bun. Spread 1 tbsp. corn mixture over each patty. Top with onion mixture and top halves of buns.

A Humble Start

Before he became John Wayne, Duke was born Marion Morrison in Winterset, Iowa. The Morrison family (below, left to right: Duke, Robert, Mary and Clyde with Duke the terrier) moved to Palmdale, California in 1914, when Duke was 7.

CHOW TIME
On the set of *The Green Berets* (1968), Duke shares a meal with daughter Aissa and the rest of the crew. Duke not only loved having his children come to the set, he would sometimes put them to work. Aissa appeared in four of her father's films, though *The Green Berets* is not among them.

NEW ENGLAND TURKEY BURGER

Caramelized onions simmered in a hoppy IPA-style beer and shaved Vermont cheddar add tang and richness to turkey meat, making these poultry-based burgers almost as flavorful as the real McCoy.

PROVISIONS

- 1   tbsp. olive oil
- 2   cups thinly sliced onion
- ¾   cup India Pale Ale
- 1   lb. ground turkey
- ¼   tsp. kosher salt
- ¼   tsp. freshly ground black pepper
- 1½   oz. Vermont white cheddar cheese, shaved
- 4   tsp. mayonnaise
- 2   tsp. whole-grain mustard
- 4   (1½-oz.) hamburger buns, toasted
- 4   small green leaf lettuce leaves
- 4   (¼-inch-thick) slices tomato

PREP

1. Heat a large skillet over medium heat. Add oil; swirl. Add onion and cook for 7 minutes or until tender, stirring every so often. Add beer and bring to a boil over medium-high heat. Reduce heat and simmer for 20 minutes or until onion is golden and liquid almost evaporates, stirring occasionally. Let it all cool.

2. Preheat grill to medium-high heat. Remove 1/4 cup onion mixture from pan and finely chop. Combine chopped onion mixture and turkey. Divide mixture into four equal portions and gently shape each into a 1/2-inch-thick patty. Press a thumb-shaped indentation in center of each patty. Sprinkle with salt and pepper. Place patties on a well-greased grill rack and grill for 5 minutes. Flip patties and grill for 3 minutes. Top with cheese and grill for 1 minute or until cheese melts and turkey is done.

3. Combine mayonnaise and mustard. Spread 1 1/2 tsp. mayonnaise mixture on bottom half of each bun; top each with one lettuce leaf, one tomato slice and one patty. Divide onion mixture evenly among servings and top with top halves of buns.

DID YOU KNOW?

In 1974, John Wayne received the Brass Balls award from the Harvard Lampoon. He arrived at the school riding an armored personnel carrier flanked by members of the Army Reserves.

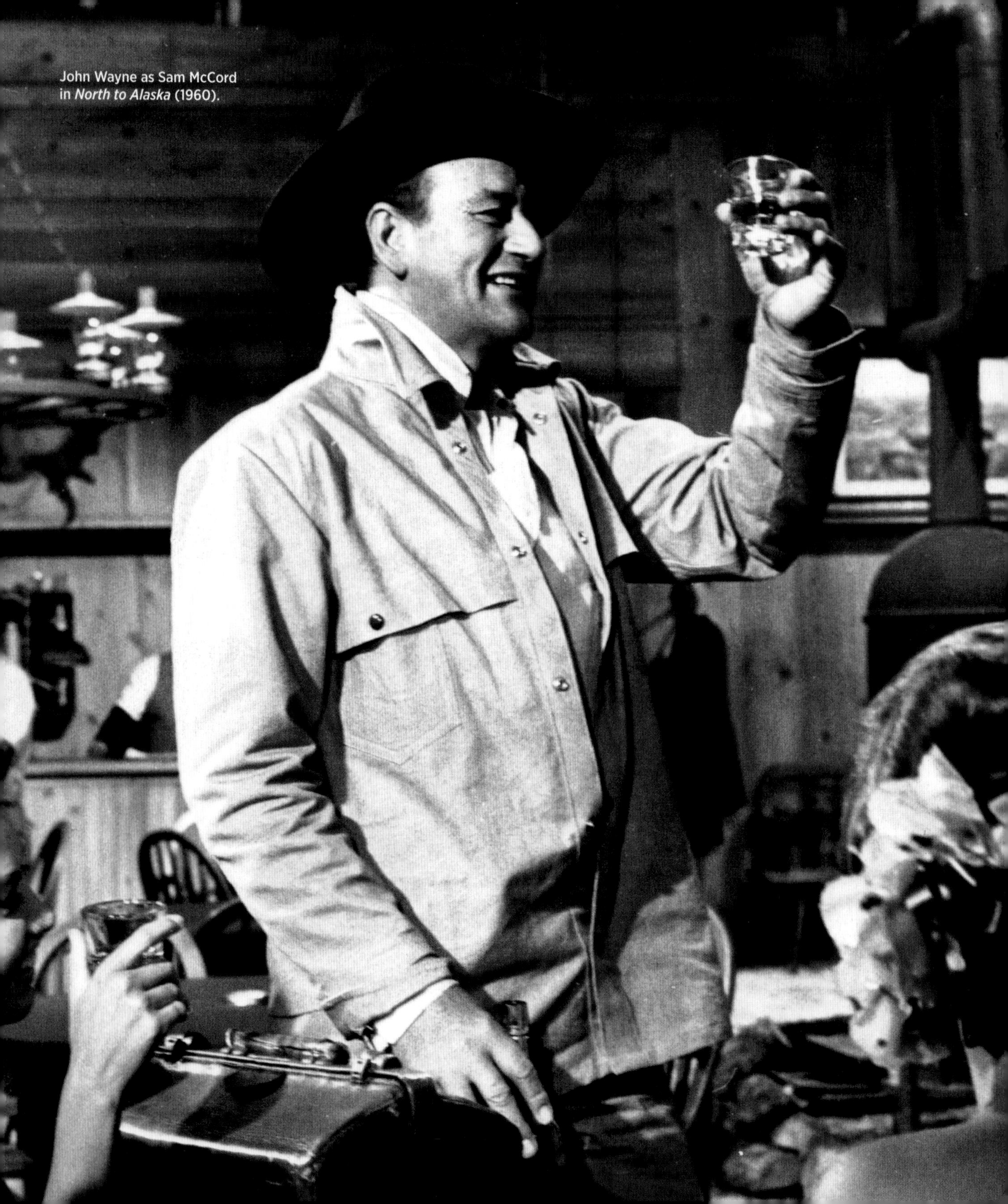

John Wayne as Sam McCord
in *North to Alaska* (1960).

BEER-BASTED SAUSAGES

Simmering sausages in beer first makes for quick grilling and rich, savory flavor. Plus, it's another reason to stock more beer.

PROVISIONS

- 6 (12-oz.) bottles heavy-bodied ale
- 12 bratwursts
- 2 large onions, cut into chunks
- Salt and pepper to taste

PREP

1. Boil beer in a large pot. Add brats, onions, salt and pepper, then simmer for about 15 minutes. Cover your mixture and remove it from heat. Set aside until you're ready to grill.

2. Heat grill to medium. Toss the sausages onto the grill using a set of tongs. Cook for about 8 minutes, turning once until both sides are browned.

3. Drain onions and serve with sausages.

Cheers To Duke

John Wayne loved a good drink as much as any man. One of his favorites was tequila served over ice he'd chipped right off a glacier while aboard the Wild Goose in Alaskan waters. He once said, "I never trust a man who doesn't drink." If you're doing so responsibly, even better.

WESTERN SAUSAGE 'N' VEGGIE KEBABS

This hearty, filling and easy-to-grill meal should be on every cowboy's menu, whether they're on the trail—or in the backyard.

PROVISIONS

¼	cup honey
½	cup spicy brown mustard
1	tbsp. soy sauce
2	cloves garlic, minced
1	jalapeño, minced
1½	lb. sausage, cut into 1-inch pieces
1	red pepper, cut into 1-inch pieces
1	onion, cut into wedges
1	zucchini, cut into 1-inch pieces

PREP

1. Heat grill to medium.

2. In a bowl, combine the first five ingredients. Add the sausage and vegetables; toss to coat. Drain marinade.

3. Thread veggies and sausage onto skewers. Put kebabs on the grill, flipping once, for about 15 minutes or until done to your liking.

The Genuine Article

John Wayne is the classic American icon, even to his own children. Duke's son Patrick says, "There's something unmistakable and indelible and, in these troubled times, maybe, when there's so much questioning about what we're doing, there's something reassuring—a moral clarity—about my father."

⚑ HOT DOG HOW-TO

Whether it's covered in chili, smothered with onions or simply accented with ketchup, mustard and a toasted bun, there are a million ways to eat a hot dog. But there are really only two ways to cook one (you know, outside of popping them in a microwave—which hardly counts). You can boil them in water or you can toss them on the grill. Since this is a grilling book and not a "things you can boil in water" book, we're gonna focus on the grilling. And you should, too. Dogs flat-out taste better when they're cooked over an open flame. It's hard to mess up a hot dog—another aspect of their popularity—but that doesn't mean it can't be done. Duke's advice is to start with a quality frank. All-natural dogs tend to have more flavor and less of that mystery juice that flows out when you cut open the package. Before you toss them on the grill, let the hot dogs reach room temperature. If you've frozen them for preservation's sake, make sure they're fully thawed: No one wants a cold dog. Once they're grilling, cook your franks on medium-low heat until they reach your desired level of doneness, then top them however you like. Feel free to use the following recipes or improvise your own style. Just be sure to make enough for a second dog per person.

California Pup

Confetti Corn

Cookout
Cruncher

Hawaiian

WAYNE FAMILY TIP

Stick a skewer in your hot dog and cut slits in it to create a spiral dog. It'll lose some juice, but your dog will be easier to cook—and it'll be a huge hit with kids.

CONFETTI CORN HOT DOG TOPPER

For a Southwest version of an all-American classic, try this topper. You'll never go back to ketchup and mustard after you've tried this combo of jalapeño and corn.

PROVISIONS

- **3** tbsp. charred corn
- **2** tsp. sliced green onion
- **1** tsp. fresh lime juice
- **2** tsp. Mexican crema
- **1** tbsp. diced red bell pepper
- **1** tsp. jalapeño slivers
- **1** tbsp. crumbled cotija or queso fresco

PREP

Combine corn, green onion, lime juice, Mexican crema, red bell pepper, jalapeño slivers and cotija or queso fresco.

CALIFORNIA PUP HOT DOG TOPPER

You don't have to be from the West to fall in love with this coastal concoction. Add it to your dog for a sweet and salty take on a familiar favorite.

PROVISIONS

- 2 tsp. mayonnaise
- 2 tsp. chopped fresh basil
- 2 tbsp. sliced avocado
- 1 tbsp. alfalfa sprouts
- 1 tbsp. sliced fresh radish
- 2 tsp. dry-roasted sunflower seeds

PREP

Mix mayo with basil, avocado, alfalfa sprouts, radish and sunflower seeds.

DID YOU KNOW?

Despite Duke's fame, his children had a normal childhood in Newport Beach, California. "A lot of times he'd pick me up from school. We could walk around town and go to Sears," Marisa says, adding that trips usually ended with popcorn or ice cream.

THE HAWAIIAN HOT DOG TOPPER

Top off your dogs island style with this pineapple- and cilantro-packed blend. You'll feel like you're feasting on the beaches of Honolulu.

PROVISIONS

- **3** tbsp. chopped fresh pineapple
- **1 ½** tsp. chopped red onion
- **1** tbsp. chopped red bell pepper
- **2** tsp. chopped macadamia nuts
- **1** tbsp. chopped fresh cilantro
- **1** tsp. fresh lime juice

PREP

Combine pineapple, onion, bell pepper, macadamia nuts, cilantro and lime juice.

DID YOU KNOW?

Hawaii was one of John Wayne's favorite vacation destinations. He also filmed a number of movies in the 50th state, parking his boat off the coast, then swimming to the set each day.

COOKOUT CRUNCHER HOT DOG TOPPER

This dog topper lives up to its name. After crunching into one of these bad boys, you'll wonder why you wasted so many years eating chip-free dogs.

PROVISIONS

- 2 tbsp. prepared coleslaw
- 3 kettle-style potato chips, crushed
- 2 tbsp. baked beans
- 1 tbsp. thinly sliced green onion

PREP

Combine coleslaw, crushed potato chips, baked beans and green onions.

COOKING LIKE DUKE

When this book ends, your supply of recipes doesn't have to.

John Wayne was an all or nothing kind of guy. He couldn't get enough of his career, his family or life in general. Duke's all-in personality transformed him into one of Hollywood's biggest stars. He appeared in more than 200 films and remains an icon today, more than 35 years after his death.

You already know about Duke's legendary work ethic and unmatchable passion. You know what he stood for, and you probably share his values. And if you're a go-getter like he was, you'll exhaust all these recipes in no time, firing up the grill at every chance, making a mark on your family's taste buds and developing a decent callous on your spatula hand. Who knows? You might even win a blue ribbon for your efforts.

But then what? Like the man said, decades into his fame, "Life's been good to me, and I want some more of it." When you've conquered all the recipes in this book, head to *MyRecipes.com* for the same classic, all-American cuisine you prepared with the help of Duke. There, you'll find more meals than John Wayne had movies.

MyRecipes.com offers visitors more than 65,000 recipes from the country's most trusted brands, including *Southern Living, Cooking Light, Sunset, Real Simple, AllYou, Health, Food & Wine* and *Coastal Living*. You'll never run out of ideas or options, even if you're as devoted to cooking as Duke was to his career. If you cooked one of their recipes per day, it'd take you nearly 200 years to master all the recipes on *MyRecipes.com*—not to mention eat them.

Best of all, the site is practical. Don't bother flipping through a table of contents; you can head straight to the search bar to seek out thousands

of recipes in seconds. Enter a meal you have in mind or search a phrase to get inspired. Want to do something with your bourbon other than drink it? No problem at all. *MyRecipes.com* has more than 500 dishes featuring different types of whiskey. Best of all, you don't need to have graduated from culinary school to cook them. Recipes are hand-picked by 50 food experts and have all been designed to be restaurant-quality, yet easy enough for any at-home chef. It's an approach that's as authentic and straight-forward as Duke was.

Plus, thanks to *MyRecipes.com*'s 25 test kitchens, eight registered dieticians and countless culinary experts, nutritionists, food scientists and chefs, when you tackle a recipe from this site, you can rest easy knowing it's going to come out right. Visitors can even create their own file of favorites, watch how-to videos, plan complete meals and do much more.

You've got the tools, you've got the drive. Now get cooking.

**UNDEFEATABLE
JALAPEÑO POPPERS**
PAGE 226

SIDES

No meal's complete without a little something on the side.
These dishes are just what you need to round out your barbecue.

Quickdraw Sauerkraut

Cast Iron Skillet Corn Bread

Brussels Sprouts and Bacon

Duke's Deviled Eggs

Classic Red Beans and Rice

Undefeatable Jalapeño Poppers

True Grits with Cheese

Backyard Coleslaw

Epic Stuffed Peppers

Old-School Creamed Spinach

Grilled Garden Medley

Scalloped Cheddar Potatoes

G.G. Corn

Supreme Pasta Salad

Duke's Macaroni and Cheese

Twice Baked Potatoes

Real Deal Baked Beans

QUICKDRAW SAUERKRAUT

Sauerkraut is the perfect topper for dogs and brats, but making it yourself can take upwards of two weeks. This pan-seared substitute is as good as the real thing and only takes 15 minutes to cook.

PROVISIONS

- 1 **Savoy cabbage, rinsed, cored and quartered**
- 2 **tbsp. canola oil**
- 1 **tbsp. mustard seeds**
- 1 **tsp. caraway seeds**
- 1 **tsp. salt**
- 1 **tsp. black pepper**
- ¾ **cup German beer**
- ¼ **cup apple cider vinegar**
- 2 **tbsp. brown sugar**

PREP

1. Add oil to a large skillet over medium heat.

2. Drop in cabbage and sauté for a few minutes until the greens have wilted slightly.

3. Add remaining ingredients to the pan and cook until the liquid has reduced by about half. The cabbage should be tender but maintain its signature crunch.

4. Store in an airtight jar until you're ready to eat. This stuff will keep for up to two weeks.

Genuine Gunslinger

He may have never worn a sheriff's badge in real life, but Duke was as proficient with a pistol as the men he brought to life on screen. "He worked that Colt single-action Army revolver and became incredibly proficient with it," says Ethan.

John Wayne stars in 1962's
The Man Who Shot Liberty Valance.

SIDES

CAST IRON CORNBREAD

This straightforward, savory cornbread is the perfect mop for baked beans—or anything soaked in barbecue sauce, really. Crumbly yet moist, it's a guaranteed crowd pleaser.

PROVISIONS

- 1½ cups cornmeal
- ½ cup self-rising flour
- 1 cup buttermilk
- 1 tsp. baking powder
- 1 (8-oz.) can creamed corn
- 1 tbsp. sugar
- ½ tsp. baking soda
- 2 eggs
- Honey

PREP

1. Combine first eight ingredients in a bowl and mix. Pour into a greased 9-inch cast iron skillet.

2. Grill, covered, for 12 minutes or until a toothpick stuck into the center of the cornbread comes out clean. Serve with honey and enjoy.

DID YOU KNOW?

In *True Grit*, John Wayne, as Rooster Cogburn, has corn dodgers—fried, baked or broiled chunks of cornbread—with him throughout the film. We'd be happy to fill our hands with that!

SIDES

BRUSSELS SPROUTS AND BACON

You'll forget anything bad you've ever heard about Brussels sprouts after trying this bacon-filled, flavor-packed dish.

PROVISIONS

- **4** strips thick-cut bacon
- **2** tbsp. butter
- **1** lb. Brussels sprouts
- **1** small onion, chopped
- Salt and pepper
- Garlic powder

PREP

1. Heat grill to medium-high. Throw bacon on the grates for 2 to 4 minutes or until crispy. Move bacon to a plate lined with a paper towel, then chop up the slices.

2. Melt butter in a skillet over high heat. Add onions and Brussels sprouts, stirring occasionally, for 8 to 10 minutes or until sprouts are golden brown. Season with salt, pepper and garlic powder to taste. Toss bacon into pan and mix a bit more before serving.

Game for Anything

Duke certainly had the appearance of a no-nonsense guy, but he had a legendary sense of humor, appearing on TV shows like Laugh-In—where he appeared wearing a bunny suit— and I Love Lucy, where he got laughs alongside his friend Lucille Ball.

WAYNE FAMILY TIP

Do you like your eggs sweet or tangy? For a sweeter deviled egg, use more mayonnaise and less mustard. If you're after a tangier taste, do the opposite.

DUKE'S DEVILED EGGS

There's the right way, the wrong way and Duke's way. When making deviled eggs, it's OK to stray from the recipe. Use ours as a base, but add more or less of whatever you want if it's to your taste.

PROVISIONS

12 large eggs

½ cup mayonnaise

2 tsp. white vinegar

3 tsp. yellow mustard

Smoked paprika

PREP

1. Put eggs in large saucepan. Fill the pan with enough water that the eggs are covered by at least 1 inch. Set pan to high heat until the water boils, then cover and lower heat. After about 1 minute, turn off heat. Let eggs sit in pan, covered, for another 15 minutes.

2. Rinse with cold water, cracking and removing shells as you go. Rinse peeled eggs to be sure that all shell pieces are gone. Dry eggs with paper towels.

3. Slice eggs lengthwise and remove the yolks into a medium bowl. Set whites aside.

4. Mix yolks with mayonnaise, vinegar and mustard until smooth. Spoon mixture into egg whites, top with paprika for flavor and presentation, then serve.

CLASSIC RED BEANS AND RICE

This hearty, easy-to-make side can fill anyone up. The only downside of this dish is ensuring you save room for your main course.

PROVISIONS

- 1 lb. red beans
- 4 cups white rice
- 1 large onion, chopped
- 2 cloves garlic, minced
- 2 bay leaves
- ½ cup bacon grease
- Cayenne pepper to taste
- Salt and pepper

PREP

1. Place beans in a round pot, add water to 4 inches above beans, soak overnight.

2. Change water. Add onion, garlic, bay leaves, bacon grease and cayenne pepper.

3. Cover and bring to a rolling boil. Reduce heat to a gentle boil and cook for 3 to 4 hours or until beans are tender and water is creamy, stirring often.

4. In a separate pot, boil the rice in about 8 cups of water, until water boils off. Let simmer for 20 minutes or until cooked.

5. Combine rice and beans in large bowl; add salt and pepper to taste.

WAYNE FAMILY TIP

For extra flavor and a taste of home, you can always add a little butter when cooking rice to the tune of about 1 tbsp. per cup. Add it after the water boils off but before it starts simmering.

SIDES

225

UNDEFEATABLE JALAPEÑO POPPERS

Spicy foods were some of Duke's favorites, so it's safe to say he would have loved this flamin' side dish. Filled with a delicious mixture of cheeses, these peppers pack the perfect punch and are sure to put some hair on your chest.

PROVISIONS

- **12 large jalapeños**
- **3 oz. cream cheese**
- **3 oz. cheddar cheese, grated**
- **¼ cup flour**
- **1 egg, beaten**
- **½ cup bread crumbs**

PREP

1. Bring grill to medium heat. Cook peppers for about 8 minutes or until evenly browned. Move peppers to a covered bowl to cool.

2. Remove the skins of the peppers. Slit each pepper just enough to remove the seeds. Mix cheeses, then stuff the pepper with mixture.

3. Roll peppers in flour, dip them in egg and roll them in bread crumbs.

4. Fry in oil until golden brown on all sides. Serve with a skewer or as finger food.

Punching Things Up

Duke was just as tough off camera as he was on screen. In his prime, he often did his own fight scenes and, with famed stuntman Yakima Canutt, created an on-screen punch method still in use today.

John Wayne stars in one of his biggest films, *True Grit* (1969).

TRUE GRITS WITH CHEESE.

These creamy cheese grits are so good that you'll never be able to go back to the normal stuff. Memorize this simple recipe, and you'll never have to.

PROVISIONS

- 8 cups water
- ½ tsp. salt
- 2 cups stone-ground yellow grits
- 2 cups shredded cheddar cheese
- 1 cup shredded mozzarella cheese
- 2 tbsp. butter
- Pepper

PREP

1. In a pot, bring 8 cups water and salt to a boil. Add grits slowly, stirring constantly to prevent clumping. Keep the grits boiling until water reduces.

2. Reduce heat to simmer. Stir in cheese, butter and pepper until well blended. Simmer on low heat for 20 minutes, stirring occasionally. Top with a little extra butter for a little extra flavor.

WAYNE FAMILY TIP

Grits go great with just about everything. Add some cooked shrimp and a few sliced jalapeños, and you'll have a one-dish meal.

WAYNE FAMILY TIP

For a creamier, lighter slaw, substitute half of your mayonnaise with sour cream. It'll give the slaw a little zip and keep it from weighing you down.

BACKYARD COLESLAW

There's no better BBQ side dish than good old-fashioned coleslaw. Not only is it a classic that everyone loves, but eating this chilled salad on a sweltering afternoon will help keep you cool.

PROVISIONS

1   head cabbage, cored and shredded

4   large carrots, shredded

3   large celery stalks, shredded

1   cup mayonnaise

¾   cup sugar

PREP

1. After shredding vegetables, combine all ingredients in a bowl.

2. Refrigerate for 3 hours, stir and serve.

EPIC STUFFED PEPPERS

If you're the type of griller who likes sides to double as a meal, you can't go wrong with these hearty stuffed peppers. Packed with ground sausage and two types of cheese, it's a vegetable any carnivore can get behind.

PROVISIONS

- 4 large peppers
- 1½ cups shredded mozzarella cheese, divided
- ¼ cup grated Parmesan cheese
- 2 tbsp. minced fresh thyme
- 2 tsp. dried oregano
- 1½ lb. ground sausage

PREP

1. Halve peppers lengthwise, removing the stems and seeds as you go.

2. Mix 1 cup mozzarella, Parmesan, herbs and sausage. Spoon mixture into halves.

3. Prepare grill for indirect medium heat using drip pan. Put peppers on grill over drip pan and cook, covered, for 30 to 35 minutes or until sausage has browned and peppers are tender.

4. Top with remaining mozzarella cheese and serve.

OLD-SCHOOL CREAMED SPINACH

You'll find creamed spinach on the menu at any great steak house, so why not pair it with the beef you grill at home? It'll become one of your dinner staples in no time.

PROVISIONS

- 4   bunches spinach (2½-lb. total)
- 2   tbsp. butter
- ½   small onion, finely chopped
- 4   cloves garlic, finely chopped
- 1   (4-oz.) bar cream cheese, softened
- ½   cup milk
-    Salt and pepper

PREP

1. Trim and wash your spinach.

2. Bring a pot of water to a boil. Add spinach and cook about 1 minute or until wilted. Drain spinach and rinse in cold water. Squeeze spinach, removing as much liquid as possible; chop and set aside.

3. In a saucepan, warm butter over medium heat. Add onion and garlic, seasoning them with salt and pepper. Cook for 3 to 4 minutes, stirring occasionally.

4. Add cream cheese and milk; stir until cream cheese is smoothly melted. Stir in spinach. Simmer over medium heat for 8 to 10 minutes or until it starts to thicken. Add salt and pepper to taste.

Ethan Wayne and Duke with newborn Marisa.

Ethan Wayne (pictured) still works to preserve Duke's memory, more than 35 years after his death.

GRILLED GARDEN MEDLEY

This basic method for grilling eggplant, tomatoes and zucchini works for other vegetables too, including green onions and bell peppers.

PROVISIONS

- 2 tbsp. salt
- 2 medium eggplants, trimmed and sliced diagonally (about ¾ inch thick)
- 2 small zucchini, trimmed and halved lengthwise
- 4 Roma tomatoes, halved lengthwise
- ⅓ cup olive oil

PREP

1. In a large bowl, dissolve 2 tbsp. salt in 3 qts. cold water. Add eggplant slices and sink them with a small plate or bowl. Let sit for 30 minutes.

2. Meanwhile, prepare grill to medium-high heat.

3. Drain and dry eggplant. Lay vegetables on a platter. Brush one side with olive oil and sprinkle with salt.

4. Brush grill with vegetable oil. Lay vegetables on grill, oiled side down. Close lid of grill and cook until grill marks form, about 5 minutes.

5. Brush dry side of vegetables with olive oil and sprinkle with salt. Turn over, close lid of grill and cook until fork tender, about 3 to 5 minutes.

6. Serve while hot.

WAYNE FAMILY TIP

There are tons of ways to grill vegetables. Try wrapping zucchini, onions, sweet potatoes and all your other favorites in foil with some olive oil, salt and pepper, then put the whole thing on the grill.

SIDES

SCALLOPED CHEDDAR POTATOES

These rich, creamy potatoes are simple to make and go great with just about any dish. It's a stick-to-the-ribs side that won't disappoint.

PROVISIONS

- **3 lb. russet potatoes, peeled and thinly sliced**
- **3 cups milk**
- **1 clove garlic, minced**
- **3 tbsp. butter, softened**
- **1 cup heavy cream**
- **8 oz. cheddar cheese, grated**
- **Salt and pepper**

PREP

1. Preheat oven to 325°. Combine potatoes and milk in a saucepan over high heat. Bring to a boil, then bring heat down to low. Cover and simmer for about 3 minutes or until potatoes are tender.

2. Drain potatoes and save the milk, making sure you have at least 2 cups.

3. Coat the inside of baking dish with garlic and butter. Add sliced potatoes and top with salt and pepper. Add saved milk and cream. Stir cheese into the potatoes.

4. Bake for about 85 minutes or until golden brown and milk has reduced and thickened.

SIDES

G.G. CORN

Duke's secretaries once referred to him as G.G., for "greatest guy." In this case, G.G. stands for garlic-grilled. This garlic- and lime-basted recipe transforms the classic ear of corn into an award-winning side dish.

PROVISIONS

- **1** tbsp. plus 2 tsp. olive oil, divided
- **2** tsp. butter
- **1** clove garlic, minced
- **4** ears shucked yellow corn
- **1** tsp. grated lime rind
- **¼** tsp. salt

PREP

1. Preheat grill to medium-high heat.

2. Put 1 tbsp. oil, butter and garlic in a small microwave-safe bowl. Microwave on high for 30 seconds or until butter melts; set aside.

3. Coat corn with remaining olive oil, arrange it on grill rack and grill for 10 minutes or until done and lightly browned, turning occasionally. Remove from grill; brush with butter mixture. Sprinkle with lime rind and salt.

WAYNE FAMILY TIP

John Wayne's secretary, Mary St. John, and her assistant and eventual successor, Pat Stacy, sent Duke a good-natured telegram in which they gave him an award of their own design. They called it the "G.G. and B.B. Award, for being the greatest guy and best boss in the world."

John Wayne steels himself for grub at Rome's Alfredo Restaurant.

SUPREME PASTA SALAD

John Wayne loved a hearty meal, and he didn't waste his time on delicate dishes. Forget lettuce salads and light vegetables. This recipe serves up veggies the way Duke would want them—in a recipe brawny enough to fill even a cowboy's stomach.

PROVISIONS

1	box tricolor rotini noodles
8	radishes, sliced
1	cucumber, quartered and sliced
1	yellow bell pepper
1-2	stalks celery, sliced
½	cup chopped broccoli
¼	cup chopped cauliflower
20	grape tomatoes
1	(6-oz.) can pitted black olives, sliced
16	oz. Italian salad dressing
2	oz. seasoned salt

PREP

1. Fill large pan with water, bring to a boil. Add pasta and cook for 9 minutes or until tender. Drain pasta. Rinse.

2. Slice vegetables. In large bowl, combine pasta, vegetables and olives. Add Italian dressing; toss until pasta, veggies and olives are well coated. Add seasoned salt; toss until veggies and pasta are well coated.

3. Cover and refrigerate for 4 hours before serving.

WAYNE FAMILY TIP

Nobody wants lukewarm food. To keep a cold side cool when serving outdoors, set your serving dish in a bigger bowl filled with ice.

SIDES

DUKE'S MACARONI AND CHEESE

Lose the elbow macaroni, pilgrim; corkscrew pasta catches more cheese than the standard noodle, making this side the genuine article when it comes to this potluck classic.

PROVISIONS

1   (8-oz.) package corkscrew pasta

4   tbsp. butter

4   tbsp. flour

1   cup milk

1   cup cream

½   tsp. salt

¼   tsp. pepper

2   cups cheddar cheese

PREP

1. Preheat oven to 400°.

2. Boil pasta in water-filled saucepan. Cook for 10 to 12 minutes or until *al dente*, stirring occasionally. Drain.

3. Melt butter in a different saucepan. Whisk in flour, salt and pepper until well blended. Add milk and cream gradually and stir constantly.

4. Bring to a boil and cook for 2 additional minutes, stirring constantly. Lower heat and cook for 10 minutes, continuing to stir. Simmer for 5 minutes, adding cheese gradually and stirring. Turn off flame.

5. Add noodles to pan and stir into mixture. Transfer to a buttered baking dish and bake for 20 minutes or until top is golden brown.

Famous Friends

Given his level of renown, it's no surprise Duke had famous friends and also had a chance to work with them. He acted alongside his pals Dean Martin in Rio Bravo (1959) and Sophia Loren in Legend of the Lost (1957).

SIDES

TWICE BAKED POTATOES

Some things are simply undeniable: *Stagecoach* changed the Western; *The Searchers* is a masterpiece; these are the best potatoes you'll ever eat.

PROVISIONS

- 6 large potatoes
- 1 tbsp. olive oil
- 1 cup sour cream
- 2 cups shredded cheddar cheese
- 1 tsp. garlic powder
- 1 tbsp. salt, divided
- ½ tbsp. pepper
- 2 green onions, chopped

PREP

1. Wash 6 large potatoes while preheating oven to 400°.

2. Poke a few holes in each potato with your fork.

3. Rub potatoes with olive oil and a little salt, then wrap them in aluminum foil. Bake for about an hour or until fork tender.

4. Remove from oven and allow to cool.

5. Cut potatoes in half lengthwise. Scoop out center of potatoes and place in a mixing bowl. Set empty skins aside.

6. Add sour cream, cheese, garlic powder, the rest of your salt and pepper to the bowl. Mix well.

7. Spoon potato mixture back into empty potato skins. Place filled skins on a baking sheet.

8. Place baking sheet in oven and bake at 350° for 20 to 30 minutes. Top with green onions and have at 'em.

DID YOU KNOW?

Duke played a lot of roles over the years, but his favorite was that of Ethan Edwards in *The Searchers*. His son, Ethan, is named after the character.

REAL DEAL BAKED BEANS

Baked beans are an old-fashioned barbecue staple and the perfect side to any grilled meat. After trying this sweet and tangy recipe, you'll be tempted to serve them all year round.

PROVISIONS

- 1 (31-oz.) can pork and beans
- ¼ cup firmly packed brown sugar
- ½ tsp. dry mustard
- 2 tbsp. molasses
- 1 onion, chopped
- ¼ cup ketchup
- 2 tbsp. cider vinegar
- 3 slices thick-cut bacon
- Salt and pepper

PREP

1. Bring grill to medium-high heat. Throw your bacon on the grates, cook until it's crisp, flipping once.

2. Combine all other ingredients in a mixing bowl. Break cooked bacon into the mixture. Stir until everything's incorporated.

3. Pour mixture into an oven-safe dish. Place dish on grill and cook for 1 hour.

4. Remove from grill, stir, serve and enjoy.

WAYNE FAMILY TIP

If your grill is otherwise occupied, these beans also work in the oven. The only difference in the end result is the consistency. Baking the beans gives them a thicker sauce.

CONVERSION GUIDE

IF YOU'RE COOKING WITH THE METRIC SYSTEM, USE THIS HANDY CHART TO CONVERT CUPS AND OUNCES TO LITERS AND GRAMS.

VOLUME

¼ tsp.	1 mL
½ tsp.	2 mL
1 tsp.	5 mL
1 tsp.	15 mL
¼ cup	50mL
⅓ cup	75 mL
½ cup	125 mL
⅔ cup	150 mL
¾ cup	175 mL
1 cup	250 mL
1 quart	1 liter
1½ quarts	1.5 liters
2 quarts	2 liters
2½ quarts	2.5 liters
3 quarts	3 liters
4 quarts	4 liters

TEMPERATURE

32° F	0° C
212° F	100° C
250° F	120° C
275° F	140° C
300° F	150° C
325° F	160° C
350° F	180° C
375° F	190° C
400° F	200° C
425° F	220° C
450° F	230° C
475° F	240° C
500° F	260° C

WEIGHT

1 oz.	30 g
2 oz.	55 g
3 oz.	85 g
4 oz / ¼ lb.	115 g
8 oz / ½ lb.	225 g
16 oz / 1 lb.	455 g
2 lb.	910 g

LENGTH

⅛ in.	3 mm
¼ in.	6 mm
½ in.	13 mm
¾ in.	19 mm
1 in.	2.5 cm
2 in.	5 cm

Cover: John Wayne: David Sutton/MPTV Images; Burger: Shutterstock; Steak: Melanie Acevedo/Getty Images. Jean Allsopp: p131, 149; Styling: Julia Rutland: p 123, 133. Ralph Anderson: Styling: Buffy Hargett: p110; Mindi Shapiro Levine: p42; William Dickey, Lisa Powell Bailey, Buffey Hargett, Vanessa McNeil Rocchio: p61. Ryan Benyi: Styling: Stephana Bottom: p185; Styling: Lynn Miller: p69; Styling: Susan Vajaranant: p90. Annabelle Breakey: p141. Jennifer Davick: p57, 64, 159; Styling: Amy Burke: 96, 101, 118. William Dickey: Styling: Lisa Powell Bailey: p39. Mark Ferri: p115. Sara Gray: p137. Brian Hagiwara: p157. Lee Harrelson: p88. Jim Henkens: p181. Beth Dreiling Hontzas: p40; Styling: Lisa Powell Bailey: 153; Styling: Cindy Barr: 58; Styling: Rose Nguyen: p52. Ray Kachatorian: p51. Rick Lew: Styling: Sara Foster: p154, 173. Becky Luigart-Stayner: p82, 92; Styling: Melanie J. Clarke: p134; Styling: Lydia DeGaris-Pursell: p239. Randy Mayor: p49, 138; Styling: Cindy Barr: p186, 190, 195, 199, 243; Melanie J. Clarke: p87; Styling: Jan Gautro: p192; Styling: Lindsey Lower: p204; Styling: Mindi Shapiro: p170. Ngoc Minh Ngo: p164. Howard L. Puckett: p126; Styling: Lydia Degaris-Pursell: p80. Lisa Romerein: p117. France Ruffenach: p145. Tina Rupp: Styling: Deborah J. Disabatino: p146. Charles Schiller: p62, 112, 183. Kate Sears: p85, 98, 175; Styling: Gerri Williams for James Reps: p169, 178. Thomas J. Story: p102. Oxmoor House: p107. Abbieimages/Thinkstock: p217. Bhofak2/Thinkstock: p15, 37. Elenathewise/iStock: p30. Joannawnuk/iStock: p215. LauriPatterson/iStock: p37. Shaiith/iStock: p202. Courtesy The Bison Company: p11. All other photos Shutterstock.

Media Lab Books would like to thank John Wayne Enterprises, custodian of the John Wayne Archives, for providing unfettered access to their private and personal collection. Best efforts were made by Media Lab Books to find and credit the photographers. Media Lab Books makes no specific claim of ownership of images contained in this publication and is claiming no specific copyright to images used.

Media Lab Books
For inquiries, call 646-838-6637

Copyright 2015 Topix Media Lab

Published by Topix Media Lab
14 Wall Street, Suite 4B
New York, NY 10005

ISBN-10: 1-942556-01-2
ISBN-13: 978-1-942556-01-5

Co-Founder, CEO Tony Romando
Co-Founder, COO Bob Lee
Vice President of Sales and New Markets Tom Mifsud
Vice President of Brand Marketing Joy Bomba

Executive Editor Jeff Ashworth
Creative Director Steven Charny
Photo Director Dave Weiss
Issue Editor James Ellis
Senior Editor Johnna Rizzo
Art Director Elizabeth Neal
Managing Editor Courtney Kerrigan
Associate Editor Tim Baker
Copy Editor Eva Saviano
Photo Editor Meg Reinhardt
Assistant Photo Editor Lindsay Pogash
Senior Designer Kyla Paolucci
Designer Bryn Waryan
Photo Assistant Kelsey Pillischer
Assistant Editor Bailey Bryant
Junior Analyst Shiva Sujan
Editorial Assistants Helena Pike, Lauren Sheffield

JOHN WAYNE ENTERPRISES

Best Wishes
John Wayne